MW00913117

HOLINESS
AND COMMUNITY

HOLINESS
AND COMMUNITY
John Coburn Preaches the Faith

JOHN B. COBURN

Morehouse Publishing
NEW YORK · HARRISBURG · DENVER

Copyright © 2010 by the Estate of John B. Coburn

All rights reserved. No part of this book may be reproduced, stored in a retrieval system, or transmitted in any form or by any means, electronic or mechanical, including photocopying, recording, or otherwise, without the written permission of the publisher.

Unless otherwise noted, the Scripture quotations contained herein are from the New Revised Standard Version Bible, copyright © 1989 by the Division of Christian Education of the National Council of Churches of Christ in the U.S.A. Used by permission. All rights reserved.

Morehouse Publishing, 4775 Linglestown Road, Harrisburg, PA 17112

Morehouse Publishing, 445 Fifth Avenue, New York, NY 10016

Morehouse Publishing is an imprint of Church Publishing Incorporated.
www.churchpublishing.org

Cover image © Yousuf Karsh
Cover design by Laurie Klein Westhafer

Library of Congress Cataloging-in-Publication Data
Coburn, John B.
    Holiness and community : John Coburn preaches the faith / John B. Coburn.
        p.   cm.
    ISBN 978-0-8192-2413-2 (pbk.)
    1. Episcopal Church—Sermons.   2. Sermons, American—20th century.   I. Title.
BX5937.C63H65   2010
252'.03—dc22

                                                                2010020733

Printed in the United States of America

10 11 12 13 14 15   10 9 8 7 6 5 4 3 2 1

Contents

An Introduction

—⚍—

John B. Coburn was called as rector of St. James' Church, Madison Avenue, in the spring of 1969. At 54, he was at the peak of a distinguished career. He was also arguably the most well-known priest in the Episcopal Church in America. Having served as president of the church's House of Deputies since the General Convention of 1967, he had already led that one thousand strong group of clergy and laity through two conventions. Previously, he had been curate of a Manhattan parish; rector of Grace Church, Amherst, Massachusetts; Amherst College chaplain; dean of Trinity Cathedral in Newark, New Jersey; dean of Episcopal Theological Seminary (now EDS) in Cambridge, Massachusetts; and was in the midst of a "gap" year, teaching at a street academy in Harlem. He had declined nomination as bishop of two different dioceses. His acceptance of St. James' call was a surprise to the church at large, if not to St. James' parishioners.

His acceptance came with a condition: one quarter of his time be devoted to his work as president of the House of Deputies, at that time, an unsalaried, part-time position. He was re-elected president in 1970, 1973, and only retired at the end of the 1976 General Convention. Thus, he held both the presidency of the House of Deputies and the rectorship of St. James' simultaneously for six years. Unable to make as many parish calls as a rector normally would, he focused primarily on hospital calls. Although the vestry had agreed to this restriction, some parishioners were disappointed and critical.

In several sermons, Coburn addressed the question of why he accepted the call to St. James'. At his institution, he preached about "The

Spirit of God in Harlem and in St. James' Church." In at least three other sermons, he sought to connect the people of St. James' directly with the people of Harlem and their needs. He substantially increased the parish's urban mission support during his six-year tenure. And by holding both leadership roles simultaneously, he helped the wider church better understand the need for increasing urban ministry throughout the country. This came at a time when many cities were in great turmoil following the death of Dr. Martin Luther King Jr., and the controversy over the Vietnam War. He believed the church and the nation had similar responsibilities. His sermon, "Theologian in the White House—The Religion of Abraham Lincoln" discussed that relationship.

Born on September 27, 1914, in Danbury, Connecticut, John Coburn grew up in an ecclesiastical family. His father, Aaron Cutler Coburn, was an Episcopal priest who had founded and was the first headmaster of the Wooster School, an independent secondary school for boys near Danbury. John attended Wooster and became valedictorian at graduation. From there, he achieved high honors in political science at Princeton, where he played varsity lacrosse and was captain of the 150-pound football team. He graduated with a bachelor's degree in 1936. At this point, his traditional path took an unusual turn. He accepted a three-year assignment to teach English and biology at Robert College outside Istanbul. Robert College was a secondary school founded by Christopher Robert, an American, to prepare able Turkish students to enter European or American universities. While at Robert College, John met Ruth, the daughter of Professor H. H. Barnum, and they were married in the Wooster School Chapel in May 1941 after the completion of his Turkish assignment.

Many years later, John advised a college student who was considering what direction his life should take that if he wanted to work for change that was deep and long lasting to choose the Christian ministry. John had pursued this path himself, entering the Union Theological Seminary in 1939 to pursue a divinity degree. Perhaps it was significant that he chose Union rather than one of the Episcopal seminaries. Union was a non-denominational, Christian, urban institution, located in New York City next to but separate from Columbia University. During John's time there it was led by Henry Sloane Coffin, and on its faculty were two of the most notable theologians of the age, Paul Tillich and Reinhold Niebuhr. Niebuhr, a famous preacher, must have been a great influence on the young Coburn, who by then had decided to follow the nonviolent path of Christian ministry rather than joining the armed forces, as so many of his Princeton friends did in wartime 1941–1942.

John graduated from Union in 1942. Upon ordination in 1943, he served as curate at Grace Church, New York City. In 1944, he was commissioned a chaplain in the United States Naval Reserve with active service in the Naval Air Station in Hutchinson, Kansas, and aboard the USS Sheridan in the Pacific theatre. He served his country for two wartime years. After this service, he was called to be rector of Grace Church, Amherst, Massachusetts, and to be chaplain of Amherst College.

Under his arrangement with the vestry of St. James', Coburn was away from the parish in July and August each year, doing his work as President of the House of Deputies or on vacation in Wellfleet, Massachusetts, his family home on Cape Cod. But most Sundays from mid-September to mid-June, he was in the pulpit at St. James', accepting very few invitations and seldom inviting others to preach. Often he would preach a series in Advent, Lent, or Epiphany. On a very few occasions— Lincoln's Birthday was one—he preached about that president who was a person he held in the highest regard.

His sermons were about twenty minutes and delivered in a characteristically calm manner. He was known in the House of Deputies as "calm Coburn, always in control." During a sermon at St. James', the baby of a young mother started to cry. As the mother got up to leave the pew with her baby in her arms, John stopped preaching and gently urged the mother to remain. She sat down, he continued preaching, and the baby stopped crying.

The subjects of his sermons were many and varied. I remember him saying that he enjoyed preaching to the church congregation week after week and that he felt sorry for bishops who had to address different parishes each Sunday. John never preached directly about the Bible lesson of the day, nor do I remember him preaching "political sermons," as many other notable preachers did in that era of unrest over the Vietnam War. Occasionally, he would start a sermon by noting a social issue, quickly moving to the personal—how to think and pray about it. He would often begin with a personal experience or a book he had read. He admired the Danish theologian Søren Kierkegaard, the secretary general of the United Nations Dag Hammarskjold, and poets Emily Dickinson and T. S. Eliot, building sermons around a message they had written.

The titles of his sermons contain words such as community, trust, passion, compassion, worship, truth, honesty, growth, affirmation, hope, covenant, commitment, love. His varied experiences enabled him to understand how people could be helped with pain, adversity, and loss. He preached about these matters as well. He had lost a child in her youth, and he wrote about her death in *Anne and the Sand Dobbies* (Seabury Press, 1964).

John used the pulpit to educate the parish about the issues of the day and how they could be approached in a non-political way. He certainly had opinions about them but was not strident, recognizing that others had differing ones. During his six years, there were two major public issues and two major ecclesiastical issues that engaged the Episcopal Church and were important for St. James' parishioners to be informed of.

John Coburn came to St. James' in September 1969, less than a year after Richard Nixon was elected President of the United States on a promise to end the Vietnam War. It was also only 18 months after the assassinations of Robert Kennedy and Martin Luther King and the riots that followed. As the war went on, opposition grew significantly. On top of this turmoil came the Watergate scandal in 1973-1974, followed by the resignation of President Richard M. Nixon. It was arguably the most divisive time the nation had faced since the years before World War II.

The other great public issue was civil rights and the urban poor, about which little progress had been made because of the Vietnam War. Urban mission became a high priority for many churches in the 1970s, including St. James'. John preached several sermons on the church's obligation to support urban mission. At his urging, St. James' purchased a neighboring building to house urban programs and hired a clergyman, Almus Thorp Jr., to develop the programs.

In the church, the movement for ordination of women had accelerated, becoming an issue at the 1967 General Convention. Among its proponents was John Coburn, in that year a member of the House of Deputies from the Diocese of Massachusetts and dean of the Episcopal Theological School. The issue did not progress far enough for acceptance, but three years later it received much wider support, particularly among the bishops. By then, Coburn chaired the House of Deputies as a deputy of the Diocese of New York. That convention authorized the ordination of women to the diaconate but not the priesthood or episcopate.

To demonstrate his convictions about the place of women in ministry, he asked a talented young deacon to join the St. James' staff in 1972. Carol Anderson fully participated in the life of the congregation except for the one sacramental act which only a priest can perform, consecrating the bread and wine at Holy Communion. Accepted by all but a few parishioners, Carol came to be greatly loved by the congregation. This appointment was widely seen by the church at large as John Coburn's full support of the ordination of women to priesthood.

In 1973, the issue again came to the General Convention and was approved by the House of Bishops but failed narrowly in the House of Deputies, where the requirement for concurrence in both the clergy and lay orders effectively amounted to a requirement for something close to sixty percent majority. Amidst bitter disappointment, delegates went home knowing they would try again in 1976.

A few women were not willing to wait. On July 29, 1974, eleven women deacons were ordained to the priesthood by three retired bishops in violation of Canon 26 of Title III, which said, "A woman may be ordained a deacon . . . etc." and was construed to mean that she could not be ordained to priest or bishop. Other deacons, including Carol Anderson, were tempted to join the "illegal 11" as they became known. John Coburn advised Carol not to be one of these, and she waited to become the first woman ordained priest in the Diocese of New York on January 1, 1977, after the 1976 convention had given its full consent, albeit on yet another close vote.

The second church issue—a revision of the Book of Common Prayer—was equally important and equally controversial. Recognizing that the Prayer Book had been revised several times since it was first published for the Church of England in the time of Archbishop Thomas Cranmer, many believed by 1970 that the time had come to revise it again. Unlike the canonical change that authorized the ordination of women, Prayer Book revision would be a constitutional change, requiring approval by two consecutive General Conventions.

The Convention of 1973, in a large step forward, authorized the trial use of a new liturgy, including an alternative Holy Communion service. It was much shorter, with more modern language and less emphasis on sin than in the 1928 Prayer Book. Some thought the new service was more authentic and closer to the practice of the ancient church. The General Convention 1973 asked all the parishes to learn about the trial liturgy and to experiment with the Communion service at appropriate times in preparation for a final decision at the 1976 Convention.

At St. James', John Coburn himself gave lectures on Sunday mornings between services about the trial or alternative service as it was sometimes called. This service was occasionally used at the Sunday morning Eucharist. Of course, there was opposition by some parishioners at St. James', as there was throughout the United States, particularly in the Southeast and Southwest and among those known as Anglo-Catholics. One of the more difficult aspects of the trial service was "the passing of the peace," where a handshake among parishioners was urged. That was new to Episcopalians and not liked by many.

During this time of learning, it became evident to the convention committee on the Prayer Book that two services would be needed. Rite I would be closer to the 1928 book. Rite II would be shorter and used on less formal occasions. At St. James', Rite I was used at 11 o'clock service and Rite II at the 9:15 service on Sundays. This seemed to be a satisfactory compromise to most of the congregation.

The General Convention of 1976, Coburn's last as President of Deputies, not only approved the ordination of women, but also gave a first approval to the new Book of Common Prayer, in spite of meaningful opposition. Three years later in 1979, it was again approved and became the only version authorized for use in the Episcopal Church. Of course, some parishes continued to use the 1928 book, but the older book is now primarily a collector's item.

Some of John's most powerful sermons were preached in the autumn of 1974, upon returning from his summer in Wellfleet. "On Riding Motorcycles" reveals his interest in Zen Buddhism and quickly moves to "caring" and "quality" of the Christian life. "Justice and Mercy" starts in an imaginary courtroom and offers "a parable about life told from a Christian perspective describing God . . . in Christ . . . in our lives." "Creative Christian Conflict" began with an account of the eleven women deacons who earlier that year had been ordained priests in defiance of the position taken by the 1973 General Convention. From this, he began a discourse on conscientious conflict and asked the question, "When we are fundamentally in deep conscientious conflict, and we know that we have to oppose one another in love, how does God make any difference?"

In "Scenes from a Marriage," he discussed how we conduct our life using the example of the Ingmar Bergman film of the same name, passages from Kierkegaard, and finally passages from the New Testament. The focus, however, was always on the individual, the person in the pew, to whom he was preaching.

On June 1, 1975, John Coburn told his Sunday morning congregation he had been elected Bishop of Massachusetts the previous day to succeed retiring Bishop John Burgess, and that he would leave St. James' in the fall, even though his consecration was to be delayed until after the 1976 General Convention. During his summer vacation, he reviewed all his St. James' sermons and was able to distill the three concepts which he examined in his September 14 sermon, "Mystery–Christ–Glory." He began by repeating the remarks he had made when he arrived six years earlier. "I am here to serve you–not on your terms or my terms–but God's . . . I hope, simply, that when I leave the life of the Spirit will be stronger."

John preached his final sermon to the congregation on All Saints' Sunday, November 2, 1975. The theme was memories, celebration, and trust. "So here we are," he said, "just as we are–with these [memories], today celebrating. There is no other word possible–celebrating, applauding, clapping our hands, our spirits applauding, celebrating with our entire beings–ourselves clapping. Because of our memories we can celebrate the present, and if we can celebrate the present, then we can look into the future with hope. Or perhaps better, we can trust the future. We can celebrate now so that we may move into the future with confidence and hope and expectancy and excitement."

And finally, "Let me conclude. Separations come in life. People we love go away, come back, go away, die. And when they go away, we die a little bit ourselves. We do, if we love them. All such little deaths are part of God's preparing us for the deaths of people we love and for our own death. These are part of life, so that together we may be raised to a new life, with new power, and renewed, eternal love surging in heaven.

When Coburn announced that he would be leaving St. James', he said the parish would be under the authority of the senior warden, C. Sims Farr, until a new rector was called. He emphasized the importance of lay leadership and said that a year or more under lay leaders would only strengthen the parish. He designated the Rev. Ralph R. Warren, assistant rector, to be in charge of liturgical matters.

In his last months at St. James', Coburn continued to follow his regular schedule. He planned the parish program for the year ahead and, with the vestry's agreement, set November 2 for his last sermon as rector. It was one of his most moving, entitled, "All Saints' Day Celebration," exploring the theme of celebrating life and trusting God. The previous month, Senior Warden C. Sims Farr had preached on "The Coburn Years and Us," concluding with the observation:

"We are then a strong team in Christ and shall go forward with exhilaration. Recognizing that this is your church then, we know you'll give it your support as you see fit. I pray for that, and thank God for the last six years."

The decision to delay consecration, which the Diocese of Massachusetts had willingly accepted, demonstrated to the whole church the importance of the upcoming convention and the decisions to be made by it on the ordination of women and the new Prayer Book, both of which were approved. He would complete his elected term as president of the House of Deputies with great distinction.

On October 2, 1976, Coburn was consecrated in the large hockey rink at Boston College. He had chosen the site, he told the September 22 General Convention *Daily*, because he wanted "to invite any Episcopalians who want to come."

John Coburn, at the age of 62, was only three years shy of the age at which many bishops retire. However, he was an active diocesan bishop of a very large diocese covering the eastern half of the state. He led this old and very prominent diocese in a distinguished way until his retirement in 1986.

He and his wife Ruth moved to Brewster on Cape Cod in retirement. John died on August 8, 2009, in his ninety-fifth year.

–Harry W. Havemeyer
Member of the Vestry of St. James' and Warden 1971–1982

Merry Christmas Pat,
with my very best wishes
Harry 2010

An Appeal for Your Life

—⚬⚬⚬—

The Twenty-Fifth Sunday after Trinity, November 15, 1970

The first draft of this sermon began like: "This sermon is an appeal for your *money*. An appeal to you to give your money away. Not all of it, but more than you ever have before and without any guarantee that you will get anything back, except the satisfaction that comes from making clear to yourself and to God what your set of values is."

I am going to read the second draft, because the first draft has been thrown away and the second draft goes like this: "This sermon is an appeal for your *life*. An appeal to you to give your life away. Not all of it, but more of it than you ever have before and without any guarantee that you will get anything back, except the satisfaction that comes from making clear to yourself and God what your set of values is."

How you spend your money determines how you spend your life. That maybe is a distortion. It may be more accurate to say that how you spend your money is probably an index of how you are spending your life.

If you want to know what your life means, how are you spending your money? You can find out very easily. Money is a part of life. It is a partial index along with other parts, it is one of many pieces. It just happens to be visible. But altogether the pieces reflect your spirit and how that life is directed by your spirit. How you spend your money, then, along with how you spend your sex life, or family life, or recreational life, or intellectual life, or cultural life, or business life, or church life—all together these various pieces express your spiritual life because finally life is all of a piece. How you spend your life is your spiritual life, of which money is a part and church is a part.

You and I, no matter how divided we may be inside or how compartmentalized we think we can carry on our life—so much for business and so much for pleasure and so much for the church—no matter how compartmentalized we think we can make our life, we are finally always one person, one body, one life, and one spirit. How that spirit possesses us is reflected in the variety of ways in the different parts of our life. What your values are, what my values are, are determined in what we pay our money for.

So an appeal, in other words, for money—an appeal to you to give away money—is really not that at all. The money in itself is not all that important. The appeal to give away your life is important.

The value of money depends upon the meaning we put to it. The value of life rests upon the meaning we give to that. If we give it away, give some of it away—if we give more of it away than we ever have before—then our life will mean more than it ever has before. The appeal is for life and within life the appeal is for money. To be generous in your giving of yourself is to give greater meaning to your whole life—the totality of your life. If that has been determined, then the money will fall into its proper place, along with your family life and your business and professional and recreational life.

It can be put the other way around. When you say a man is stingy because he does not give money—a man who says, "I do not believe in charity," you say *he* is stingy. You say his spirit is stingy. That is the kind of man he is. He is stingy all over, in all aspects of his life. He wants to hold on to everything that he's got or direct traffic according to his rules—wanting his way all the way. So, of the generous man who gives freely of his money, we say not simply that he has a generous spirit, we say, *he* is a generous man.

An appeal will come to you this week for the support of the work of the church. The importance of the appeal is in the giving of ourselves in a generous spirit to life itself: in a generous spirit to our family or to our associates, our neighbors and because we have money, to the poor who are our neighbors. How you spend your money is a parable of how you spend your life. It is very down to earth, which is why Jesus used parables to teach about life.

A man was once given $5,000, and he invested it. Some time later the man who gave him the $5,000 came back and said, "How much do you have?" He said, "I have $10,000." He replied, "That is a good job you did." Another man at the same time was given $2,000. He turned it into

$4,000. When the donor asked him what he had done, he said, "I have now doubled your money." He said, "That is a fine job you have done."

Then he went to the third man to whom he had given $1,000. He asked, "Well, what did you do with the money?" He replied, "I was afraid. I was afraid that I might not succeed and that you would hurt me. So I put the money in a safe deposit vault and here is the $1,000." And the donor said, "You are a fool. You are just plain stupid to act like that. You are never going to get anywhere in life if you are fearful all the time. If all you ever do is to be concerned about your own skin, if that is the way you are going to live, you are finished." So he took the $1,000 and gave it to the man who had the $10,000 and remarked, "That is the way life is, brothers. If you've got it, you had better invest it. Everybody has something and if you don't invest it, it's taken away. That is the way life is." So that man curled up and died—just like everybody with that type of spirit. We can't play it safe. We can't take it with us. We can't get anywhere by hoarding.

The talents—they have to be invested. Both money and life. Of course, it is a gamble because, until you put your money down, you do not know whether it is going to come back. You can look and see that people who never put their money down die in their spirit.

So it is a parable. It is more about life than it is about money. As they say, the crunch is where the money is. Your life, your talents, your gifts, they are given. They are given to be used. If you use them, they will grow. If you do not use them, they will dry up. Give your life outward with courage—you will get hurt but you will thrive. Back away, protect, keep, hoard—you will die.

This is true of personal talents: the ability to play the piano or to sing. It is true of the gifts of the intellect. It is true of religious gifts, the gift of faith. It is a great mystery, some people believe and other people do not. The tragedy is not with the people who do not believe if they have not been given that gift. The tragedy is with the people who have been given that gift and then never act on it. That is death.

It is true of the gift of our heritage, any heritage: the gift of our nation, the gift of a city, the gift of a church—guard it, protect it, put soldiers around it, do not let anybody have any share in it, and one day it is gone. It is true of the gift of the gospel. It is the same thing. Give it away and it flourishes. Hold on to it for ourselves—it disappears. The gospel *demands* that it be given away; that is to say life demands that it be given away. This is what the gospel and life are all about: God giving himself away. Not just once, but day after day after day, he is giving himself away in love for you and for me. We in response then are willing to give ourselves away, or to give ourselves more away each day.

That is the only way love and compassion and caring can ever be spread. That is the only way that the spears will be broken and that peace will come. So if you hold the gospel and protect it and refuse to share it, it disappears. Then the church is left only with the church, an ecclesiastical organization to support. There is no life there. There is no gospel.

So the appeal is not for the church as an institution for your life. The appeal is for the gospel, the grace of a free spirit. That is different from holding on. It is the sparkle of a young child who gets an overcoat or who learns the alphabet, or who takes an excursion with his friends. That is different. That is healing. That is life. That is the gospel. The church may be a vehicle for that gospel.

All this is simply to say that your life, in a way, will depend upon how you give. Not how much you give—nobody can determine that except you and God—but *how*, you give, with what spirit.

It is important then to use both the first draft and the second: to appeal for your money, for this is the way that Christ appealed for your life. Amen.

The Ministry of
St. James' People

—∞—

The Third Sunday in Advent,
December 13, 1970

The best way to answer the question, "What does the Episcopal Church believe?" is to say, "Read the collects." These are the prayers of the church, a different prayer for each Sunday of the Church Year, and taken all together they declare the belief that the Episcopal Church has in God. So the collects in Advent are preparation for God's coming.

The first Sunday in Advent's collect presents a theme which is carried on through all four weeks of Advent. All life—the shadows and the dark places as well as the light and the brilliant places—all life is to be prepared for Christ's coming. Don't therefore try to exclude part of your life in preparation for Christmas. Don't put aside temptations or the passions or the pain or the sorrow or the burdens or the deaths. Don't try to put aside any of those parts of your life that you are not happy with. Rather include them in the affirmation of all of life being prepared for God's coming. As you think of that Christ child coming into your life, think of him as the one who may pull together all the loose strings into one whole. So do not hide or do not try to pretend but open everything.

The second collect about which Mr. Warren preached last week has as its theme the Bible. Christian people are waiting for God to come again. They have a history which is described in the record of those early people of God written in the Bible.

There is a record there of how God prepares the hearts of people for his coming, not just once but generation after generation, year after year after year. If you would prepare yourselves now, it will be in the same old way that the people have always been prepared: the way of honesty, of confessing failure, of confessing our concern for ourselves before our concern for our neighbors; acknowledging that from the deepest well-springs of our life, we do want to be more honest, more open and more loving and more forgiving and more just—more committed, more really committed to the forces of righteousness that we see around us. It is in that kind of a spirit that we are reminded Christ comes.

The third collect today has exactly the same theme, but this time it concentrates upon the place of the ministry in helping the people of God prepare for his coming. The task of ministry, says the collect, is to help the people prepare for Christmas by having their hearts opened more, that their actions may be more just, so that they may be strengthened to live in that spirit of Christ when he comes in their lives in the world.

This sermon is about this ministry and this ministry in relation to God's people. As Mr. Warren related the Bible to the church school program of St. James' Church last week, let me attempt to make reference to the people of God in St. James' Church this week and to the ministry that we hold in common.

Now if you are a stranger to St. James' Church and do not intend to ever come back again, you are welcome to any free wisdom that you want to take back to your parish or if you would like to take a snooze, this would be a good time.

There are three things I want to say, all from the Biblical perspective. The basic unit of Christian living is the congregation. It is not the clergy; it is the congregation. It is the people of God who are gathered together. The apostles were first gathered together around the table. When they went out, they went to establish other little congregations which would gather together around tables and remember Jesus. That is what they did in Ephesus and Corinth and Salonica and Rome and all through the Mediterranean world. That has always been the thrust of the church, of the life of a congregation—moving out to establish other congregations that other people might remember Jesus. It is always expanding. It has always been mission minded. It has always had to do with the estab-lishment of new life for new people in new gatherings that they may have something of the vigor and the vitality of people who know that God is God and Christ is their Lord.

Ministers were chosen in very early times in a variety of ways, but they were always chosen by the congregation and very largely from amongst themselves in order that they might have someone who on their behalf would break the bread in memory of Christ and would preach the gospel. The Communion and the gospel is the combination of *inward* nourishment and strength to go *out* and let the world know who Christ is. They were the servants of the congregation. The ministers therefore were called to serve the people in order that their hearts might be prepared for God's coming day after day, so that all people outside the church might know. So the first point is the basic unit which has always been the local congregation, and it always will be because that is where people meet together around the table and hear the gospel.

The second point is this. During the latter part of the Middle Ages and the Reformation, in both the Catholic and the Reformed tradition, the church began to turn inward. The outward thrust was blunted and the vitality began to diminish. This turning inward was symbolized by the almost absolute emphasis upon either the priest breaking the bread for the people or the reformed preacher preaching the Word for the people—for them alone, for those who already belong, in order that they might be comforted in their own life rather than for service to all men. Priests and ministers were engaged to please the people rather than to serve them as ministers of the gospel. That tide is now running out. It is running its course. It has been running out for a hundred years in western culture. The church concerned about itself is inevitably losing ground. In Friday's paper you may have seen the notification that one half of the national church's staff at 815 Second Avenue is being dismissed because there is not enough money. When a church has accumulated generations of primary concern about its institutional life, it always runs out of money. Unless that tide is reversed and the gospel taken by the people to the people outside the church, the funds will continue to diminish. The vitality of a Christian church can almost always be determined by its concern for those who stand outside the church rather than for those who stand within the church. There are exceptions— the Fundamentalists that have made such an extraordinary growth, tending by and large to stress the next life to the neglect of this life, and splinter groups that have broken off into small groups of meetings and formed part of what is called "the underground church" for the renewal of the church. So the second point is to identify a trend of what happens when the inward look is the exclusive look.

Thirdly, we now stand in the middle of this transition period from the nineteenth century to the twenty-first century when Christ will be coming again. He will be coming then as he is coming now. How are we in this congregation preparing for his coming? How are we preparing for his coming in this year that we may have our hearts prepared for his coming every year so that when he comes, he may come with power?

There are two keys. One is the opening up of congregational life. The central unit of the parish is the congregation, and everything the vestry has been doing these recent months has been directed to have their committees so restructured that more and more people in the life of the congregation may participate in the decisions that affect the life of the congregation.

They have begun to grapple with questions like, "What shall we teach our children, and how? What is the best way to worship God in this place of beauty, and why? Who should use our Parish House during the week? How should we spend our money? What proportion should be spent on our house-keeping, and what proportion should be spent for others? How should we raise our money? What proportion of the people should be expected to participate in the giving to the work of the church? How can we come to a deeper understanding of ourselves in some way that complements our services of worship. What is the purpose of the church and what may we do to carry it out?" In these ways and others the vestry and lay people are already working.

The second key of course is that one already mentioned, the necessity for a congregation in whatever era—the first century or the fifteenth century or the twentieth century—to be outward looking. This is to be community oriented, to have a responsibility for the work of the diocese, to be concerned about the national church. It is to be concerned about the churches in our community as well as the people in our community.

We are going, I believe, in the right direction. Much of this has been going on for generations in this parish. Some of it is new to our thinking. All of it is probably more self-conscious than it has been. The ministry is given by God to enable the people of God—that is, the ministers here are given by God to prepare the people of God here—that they may live a life worthy of God's gospel. It is not for the people to support the ministers in their ministry, it is for the ministers to support the people for Christ's coming. Ministers therefore are given by God to bring you encouragement on the way, that you may turn in an outward direction with hope, with expectation and with joy because you know that God is God and Christ is the Lord and therefore there may be nothing to be afraid of in your personal life or your national life—it is all in God's life.

I want to conclude with an analogy I hope you will not take literally, but seriously. Last week there was a little procession on Fifth Avenue outside Altman's Department Store, a primary school class of twenty-five three- and four-year-olds and three teachers. They lined up outside the door and each teacher told each one to take another by the hand. So they walked in two by two, having been admonished to remain very quiet when they went through the aisles.

They went to the escalator and began to go up to, I think the sixth floor. As they began to leave the fourth floor, one child began to sing "Jingle Bells, Jingle Bells, Jingle All the Way." By the time they reached the sixth floor the whole class was singing and everybody visible was singing "Jingle Bells." Then they quieted as they stood in line to meet Santa Claus. As they lined up each one went forward in turn. He was a wonderful Santa Claus. He reached out and put his arms around each child, and he held him. He listened to him and said a word. Then the child went away with his face absolutely radiant.

That child's world was going to be better for his presence in it because he had been lifted by Santa Claus. Our world is meant to be better because we have been lifted by Jesus Christ in the midst of his people. Amen.

Decisions—and a Promise

—m—

Fourth Sunday after Epiphany,
January 31, 1971

This sermon is about decisions—decisions that you make that make a difference. It is about the few fundamental decisions that you make that turn out to be turning points in your life. They are decisions that change direction for you.

You say as a young man, "I will become an engineer rather than a poet." You say to one girl rather than to another, "Betty, I want you to marry me." And life hasn't been the same since then.

You say, when your wife Betty dies, "I will now do this." You come to the end of a dead-end job and you say, "I will do something to make my life count."

So this sermon is about these few critical decisions. Not about the many daily routine decisions—although they are just as important in the long run. Decisions like, "why get up in the morning?" Or "why go home at night?" Those are for another sermon.

To get a perspective for our thinking on these decisions let me ask you to look at that first decision that Jesus made about how he was to spend his life, how he announced that decision in the lesson that was read this morning from the New Testament (Luke 4:16–32).

It was his first appearance as an adult in his hometown, and it was there that he made his decision openly.

He had lived in Nazareth as a child. He had grown up there. He stayed there as a young man assisting—according to tradition—his father, a carpenter, for thirty years.

Then, after he had been baptized by John the Baptist, he went into the wilderness to wrestle with the question of his vocation, and he came to a decision.

He was going to teach the Kingdom of God—repent and believe and the Kingdom of God will be ushered in. So he began to go through the countryside, teaching, as was the custom in those days, in the synagogues. When he came to Nazareth he was invited to attend the synagogue, to read from the Scripture, then to interpret the passage.

The Scripture for that day was that passage that was read from the Old Testament lesson (Isaiah 61). The lesson of God to his people in exile.

The Spirit of the Lord is upon me,
because he has anointed me to preach good news to the poor.
He has sent me to proclaim release to the captives
and recovering of sight to the blind,
to set at liberty those who are oppressed,
to proclaim the acceptable year of the Lord.

Then he closed the book. The people looked at him and he said, "Today, this Scripture is fulfilled in your hearing."

This means that God's Kingdom is for all people—not just for us who are Jews. This (to them) blasphemy caused them to take him, and, as we would say, ride him out of town. Luke says, "He went away."

Now let me ask you to think about that decision—of what he was going to do with his life—of how it may cast some light upon our decisions, what lay behind it—the decision itself and what happened.

What lay behind it was very simply thirty years. The so-called "hidden years" of Jesus' life, when he did not do anything out of the ordinary; he just grew up.

Influences were at work on him during those hidden years.

That fundamental influence of his family, as that influence in any child growing up, is his family. He saw how his mother and father treated each other. He expressed the security of a family that "hung together" in a certain way, whose members treated each other in a certain way.

Young people get insights as to who they are as they observe their mother and father treating each other. We can frequently get insights into what a family is like as we observe how brothers and sisters feel about each other. It is a "hidden" kind of influence. Words do not mean very much. Feeling, treating, touching, commitment—these mean everything. Who stands for what? A child knows what his family stands for without it ever being said to him.

Jesus had that hidden influence of his family and of his synagogue in school. In those days those two were together. What his father believed and what his forefathers believed provided the raw material of his education, so he came to know what he believed. The history of God's search for men is the history of the people of Israel; the evidence of that search and the promise of what was held out was for those who had some sense of belief. In other words, there was the influence again in a hidden way.

What other influences you can describe as well as I on the basis of your own experience.

The point is simply that all of these influences are hidden. They are in the background—they are the backdrop for the decision that is about to be made openly. They are quiet, very ordinary, very routine, simply human stuff. Not much happens. Not much is meant to happen. The preparation for a decision is always waiting quietly and hiddenly.

Robert Frost used to take a month a year in residence at Amherst College talking to students and faculty in a very informal way, usually the later at night the better for him. One night in a fraternity house a sophomore said to him, "Mr. Frost, what is the best combination of courses to take to get a good education in Amherst College?" Mr. Frost looked at him and said, "Well, you know it doesn't make any difference—it doesn't make any difference what you take. Take anything under the sun that you want to take, and after a while you catch on—or you don't. But it doesn't depend upon the courses. It depends upon your just hanging around." So for thirty years Jesus "hung around" Nazareth. That is what we do most of the time in our lives, preparing for decisions by just hanging around the place.

The time of decision is always determined. It is not determined by us. It is determined by the Spirit. It is when there is an overpowering sense of urgency and fulfillment when one knows with all one's being what that decision is meant to be.

The phrase quoted by Jesus is "the Spirit of the Lord is upon me." These decisions of the spirit are always "spirit-filled" decisions. They may be rational, but they are more than reason. They may be ethical but they are more than ethics or morality. They are decisions not so much that one makes but that one participates in, that one consents to. They are made by the spirit and we participate in that decision. They do not come often but they change one's destiny.

A student in a seminary in 1965 was hanging around, waiting to be able to make a decision about going to Selma. He describes how that decision was made. He writes, "My soul doth magnify the Lord and my spirit hath rejoiced in God, my savior. I had come to an evening prayer as usual that evening and as usual I was singing the Magnificat with that special love and reverence I have always had for Mary's glad song. He hath showed strength with his arm. As the lovely hymn of the God bearer continued, I found myself peculiarly alert, suddenly straining toward the luminous Spirit-filled 'moment' that would, in retrospect, remind me of others . . . Then it came. 'He hath filled the hungry with good things!' I knew then that I must go to Selma."*

It is at a time like that when you know what you must decide—that the spirit decides. Your spirit. You and the Spirit decide. "Yes" or "no." No "ifs," "ands" or "buts." When the Spirit is about his business it is "yes" or "no." You know. The decision is yours. It is clear, and your life is never the same again after that kind of a decision.

Now there is one final characteristic about decisions of this kind. It has to do with what happens next, after a clear "spirit-filled" decision is made. What happens next is always different from what you think is going to happen next. Someone said, "life is what happens to you when you are making plans."

Jesus thought all he had to do was to gather some disciples to teach them; they would teach the people about God's Kingdom; and together they would help bring it in. What happened was that his disciples ran away; he was left alone to usher in God's Kingdom. And he did it not by his teaching but by his death; not by his success but by his failure; not by the power he had but by no power. The spirit which filled him on that day when the decision was made—that spirit was set loose in the world of men because something different happened from what he thought was going to happen. That is the difference that it made. The spirit was moved out into the lives of men.

The boy who went to Selma to establish justice between races was killed by a white man and nobody who ever knew that boy will ever be the same again. He did not expect to be killed. What happened was something quite different from what he thought would happen.

The spirit moved on and touched others. He passed the spirit on. Now some people live in that spirit who never knew the spirit.

Nobody can tell you when your moment of decision comes except you and your spirit. When it comes it always sets you free. When you

---

*The reference is to Jonathan Myrick Daniels, whose feast day is observed in the Episcopal Church on August 14.

make that decision you know you are free and that nothing else makes any difference. What happens won't be what you expect; it will be better. That is the promise of the spirit.

Saying "yes" to the spirit never fails. That is a promise—it is Christ's promise. It is a promise that every man makes who has ever lived in that spirit. It is a promise that you make yourself every time that you have said "yes" to the spirit.

It is a passing of the spirit on. Men are set free as the spirit is passed on—set free in ways we never dream of, set free in the lives of people whom we never meet. It is the great mystery.

So wait, go about your business, hang around, be quiet, be expectant and open to the spirit—then when the moment comes—given by that spirit—then decide with all your being. What happens will be greater than you can imagine.

That is a promise—it is a promise of the spirit.

Let us pray.

America! America!

—∿—

The Fourth Sunday in Lent,
March 21, 1971

This sermon is prompted by the recent deaths of two great Americans: Thomas Dewey and Whitney Young. It is a sermon about America, and its text is "In God We Trust."

> O beautiful for spacious skies,
> For amber waves of grain,
> For purple mountain majesties
> Above the fruited plain!
> America! America!
> God shed his grace on thee,
> And crown thy good with brotherhood
> From sea to shining sea.

The funeral service for Governor Dewey, held in this church on Friday, concluded with the singing of this hymn. It wove together, in an extraordinary fashion, the strands that were in that service; the life of a man dedicated to serving his country by—among other ways—his serving the integrity of the law of the land; by the presence of the President, members of his Cabinet, the Senators of this State, the Governor, the Mayor, the elected representatives of the people of America; and by the affirmation in that service that our final trust—in life and in death—is in God.

In parentheses I should like to say that the way in which the special service representatives from the White House conducted themselves for two days in this church and parish house was a credit to the central symbol of American life that is the White House. They conducted themselves with dignity, with courtesy, with respect for the traditions of the church, and with great efficiency. And for those of you who sometimes get discouraged about New York, let me say that the same things were true of the police on every level. It was, for us here, a great lesson in human behavior, expressed with order and respect for one another, always with courtesy.

The gathering on that day of what might be called the Establishment, the political Establishment in America, was not only a testimony to the integrity of Governor Dewey, but also to his own conviction that it is the integrity of the law that provides the roots for a stable society that can themselves only bring liberty and justice for all. Without the inner moral integrity in law which makes justice possible, then the health of a society begins to erode. That requires—the preservation of the moral integrity of the law requires—hard work, an acknowledgement of and correction of injustice, and self-discipline.

> O beautiful for pilgrim feet,
> Whose stern, impassioned stress
> A thoroughfare for freedom beat
> Across the wilderness!
> America! America!
> God mend thine every flaw,
> Confirm thy soul in self-control,
> Thy liberty in law.

There is no liberty apart from law. Law is preserved through "stern, impassioned stress" generation after generation by the continual mending of "every flaw" in our national life and by our daily confirming our souls "in self-control." These are the ways by which the moral integrity of the law is preserved, and which provides the roots for a healthy society.

On Wednesday there was another funeral for another great American: in Riverside Church, Whitney Young. The way in which he dedicated his life to America said: "The law has to keep on growing in order that there may always be more justice, more liberty, more equality for more people under the law, if society is to flourish and be strong. Law which stays the same stultifies and finally destroys."

So he worked within the Establishment to change it. He worked within the law—to change it. He gave himself to America—to change it.

The funerals of these two great Americans in this week bring then this first reflection about America. It is only as the law is obeyed that it retains its integrity, and it is only as it changes that it retains its integrity. Its purpose is to bring greater justice and liberty for more and more Americans.

Now the second reflection is this: It is in the form of a question. Why is it necessary for death to bring about reflection? Why does death bring with it a deeper dimension to our everyday reflection than we normally have?

Even a natural death at the end of a man's three score and ten years brings an opportunity for reflection upon his life that we do not get during his lifetime. The meaning of his life usually cannot be fully understood until he has died. And when a man's death is not natural, but violent, the reflection sometimes brings with it a conviction that brings change that would not otherwise have come. The deaths of John Kennedy and Robert Kennedy and Martin Luther King have brought profound changes in the way America reflects about its society.

But there is no power for change so powerful as that which comes through sacrificial death: the voluntary giving of one's life for another, or for one's country. A man's life counts for most when he believes in something so much, he is willing to die for it.

This is a voluntary offering that has such power. A man is willing to die because his cause is right, or his country's cause is right. So Americans from Bunker Hill to Iwo Jima have brought strength to their country by their willing self-sacrifice for their country's cause, which they have known to be right. That is health; that is power for a society. That holds a society together with strength.

And one reason for our current disease in our society is clearly because so many Americans are uneasy about whether the cause in southeast Asia is right. They ask: is that sacrifice consistent with the greatness of America, with those sacrifices that have made America great?

> O beautiful for heroes proved
> In liberating strife,
> Who more than self their country loved,
> And mercy more than life!
> America! America!
> May God thy gold refine,
> Till all success be nobleness,
> And every gain divine.

Change comes when men are willing to lay down their lives to preserve the moral integrity of society. Change comes when men are willing to lay down their lives for their vision of what that society might become.

> O beautiful for patriot dream
> That sees beyond the years
> Thine alabaster cities gleam,
> Undimmed by human tears!

That "patriot dream" is translated, "In God We Trust." Americans say that. They say that on the very symbol of what many who distrust America consider to be its flag, the dollar bill. It's written right there. Our trust is not in the dollar bill. It is in God. It is not in what money buys—power—it is in God. Americans say our trust is not even in America—it is in God in America.

And to the debunkers who say "that's only a dream," Americans can say, "It is no dream—it is as real as the life and death of Thomas Dewey and Whitney Young—as real as the flesh and blood of ordinary men and women who in their daily lives try to live out their own lives with moral integrity, who are obedient to the vision of an America with moral integrity whose trust is in God and in this vision of what the cause of America should be: of a nation to serve all nations, to serve the brotherhood of all men. So the law changes, society changes, that there may be greater liberty in the law for all mankind.

> America! America!
> God shed his grace on thee,
> And crown thy good with brotherhood
> From sea to shining sea. Amen.

Almighty God who hath given us this good land for our heritage, in the time of prosperity fill our hearts with thankfulness, and in the day of trouble suffer not our trust in thee to fail through Jesus Christ, our Lord. Amen.

A Community of Trust

—⚍—

The Fifth Sunday after Easter,
May 16, 1971

This is the first of two sermons about St. James' Church. They are prompted by the parish meeting which will be held next Sunday and are meant to provide preparation and perspective for that meeting and for our life together.

The sermon this morning has to do with our internal life and the one next week about our external life. The one this morning is entitled, "A Community of Trust," and the one next week (unless it gets changed during the week), "A Church with a Mission." This division between internal and external is of course an artificial one. The spirit that binds people together is always expressed in what they *do,* and what they do is determined by the ways in which they decide what to do. Internal structure, in other words, and external purpose are part and parcel of the common life of any group of people.

Let me begin with an analogy. Let us imagine that you are a parent and you want to give your children the essentials for constructive living. What would be the most essential quality you would like them to have?

A case can be made that the one quality that will stand them in greatest stead in the long run will be their integrity. Perhaps the greatest contribution that we can make to American society is to give our children to that society as adults who become trustworthy citizens.

I have been struck in recent weeks by a very common note sounded by different kinds of people who are searching for a leader: a company searching for a new president, a secondary school looking for a new headmaster, a college looking for a new president. All groups given the assignment to find a man who would lead them have all said there is one essential quality to begin with. The first quality the man must have, they have all said, is natural, spontaneous, absolute integrity. They want, above all, a man who can be trusted.

How do you set about producing trustworthy children? Well, as a husband and wife, first of all, trust each other, as they give each other freedom to be themselves, "to become their own person." In that climate of trust, then, children grow trustworthy, as they are trusted. If you do not ever trust them, how can they ever grow in trust? Have you ever had your child say, "The problem is you don't really trust me, do you?" Then you can reply, "Well, yes, I trust you—within limits. But right now you are not old enough, or intelligent enough, or responsible enough to be trusted in every area of life so I trust you within certain limits. But I intend to trust you finally, without any limits whatsoever. Those limits will disappear. To grow in trust takes time." The greater the trust given as the child grows, the limits made wider and wider, the greater the trustworthiness given by the adult to his society.

Well, this is an imperfect analogy. But as the family sets the climate of trust within which a child grows into a trustworthy adult, so the parish sets the climate within which its members grow to trust one another and—in that trusting—trusting the spirit of God who has brought them together in this way, the church may make its mature, trustworthy contribution to the society of which it is a part. If it cannot make that contribution then it has little contribution that it can make.

The parish can be thought of as a Christian family within which members learn to trust one another, to trust life, to trust God, to trust his spirit, so that they may do his work, carry out his mission.

There are three things that can he said, I believe, about that trust. The first is this: *trust is always a by-product*. It comes up alongside people. It can never be developed directly. It never can be compelled. No one can ever be forced to trust. It comes as a by-product of people working together on a common task. As they reveal themselves, in doing that work, to be trustworthy and become increasingly trustworthy, then the spirit of trust gradually appears. It is just there.

In the life of parishes, therefore—and this is the second thing that can be said—*the place to begin is in its work*. What do the people do? What is the church there for? Why are they members of it? What purpose does it serve?

Who decides that? What are the criteria used to make the decision? What weight is given to the tradition of a parish or the needs of the people, or the needs of the community?

What, in a word, is it up to? Why is St. James' Church here on Madison Avenue and Seventy-First Street? Is the mission of the church to build the church? If it is to announce by its words, and its life and the way it uses its building, and the way it raises money and spends money, the good news that Jesus is raised from the dead and the Lord of all life—what does that mean? Who decides what it means? What are the issues that are important in the life of the parish?

How to stay alive? How to raise money? How to repair the roof? (Our roof is leaking this morning over the north aisle.) How to ease racial tensions? How to make public school education better? How to keep rats out of cribs? How to deal with drugs for children? Whose children?

The point is, I trust, a clear one: Trust rests upon the way people respond in working together to meet the needs that they have, the needs of the parish and needs of people outside the parish.

The third thing that can be said is that *the structure of a parish*—that is, the ways by which decisions are made and programs carried out—in fact *determines what the task is thought to be.* Structures are always necessary to help people relate to each other and carry out their work. Some structures prevent people from participating together. The clearest illustration is in the traditional parish structure where the authority is lodged in a body called "Rector, Wardens and Vestry" and its authority is absolute. That body decides what the mission of the church is, and then it tells the people. Program is decided by that body, and the people are asked to finance it. They are recruited to carry out decisions made by the "Rector, Wardens and Vestry." The authority is always from the top down.

More than that, it is from the clergy to the laity. The first named official of the church is the rector. "Rector" means "ruler." He "rules" his people. It is *his* ministry the people are expected to support. The vestry urges the people to be loyal to the ministry of a particular rector. They are called upon to carry out his ideas.

This may be a slight caricature of the parish and the Episcopal Church. It is not as true today as it was yesterday, but it is still more true than it is false. It is as true as it is wrong. It makes it impossible for a community of trust ever to be developed. There may be loyalty to a person, a rector, or to the clergy, but as long as the structure divides the clergy from the laity so that the laity are expected to carry out the clergy's ministry, then it is impossible for a spirit of trust to be developed. Trust comes when clergy and laity work together in the carrying out of a common task, determined by clergy and laity, both in its goal and in its execution.

The reason for these comments is that in an effort to make that spirit of trust more easily developed as a by-product in this parish, the vestry has taken leadership in modifying that structure. Next week's parish meeting is one illustration. Furthermore we have now completed one year in this parish, of living with structural changes which have not only made new directions possible about the essential work of the church but have made it possible for decisions about those directions to be made in new ways. And in many instances they have been made to widen and deepen the sense of participation and therefore the climate of trust. They have done so by identifying what it is a parish does—and then having clergy and laity together plan and act. Not just the vestry but vestry committees open to members of the parish. This is another illustration.

What does a parish do? Well, it *worships*. How it worships is determined by the people and the clergy together in order that we may have the best of the people, in order that this may be a common act as powerful, as relevant, and as wholly as possible. This is done through a worship committee.

A parish also *learns*. It learns the truth of the gospel of Christ. We learn it differently than our forefathers learned it. But it is the same truth. How we learn it is determined by an education committee made up of ninety-nine percent lay men and women.

A parish also *meets* together. It meets not in large impersonal groups but in small groups. So there is a pastoral committee that provides opportunities for persons to meet persons and to share a common fellowship. This is to make it possible to appropriate the truth of the gospel in personal terms, else it is only academic learning.

Finally a parish *serves* human needs. So there is a community committee which makes decisions on how we can intelligently and imaginatively be helped to love our neighbor as ourselves—just as ourselves.

So that is the direction in which the internal structure of this parish is taking us. There are vestry committees for all people—reflected also in the emerging structure of the women's association. There are greater numbers of people participating in decisions and in the work of the church.

We do not do it terribly well but we are doing it moving with a good spirit in this direction. We will never do it perfectly but as we learn to trust the spirit moving among us we shall better be able to do what he wants us to do and that trust will grow.

The church is a family—with different members doing different things, having different points of view, performing different functions but bound by a common spirit of trust.

As we work together as members of that family trying to act in accordance with that spirit—even when we are not quite sure what that spirit wants us to do, even when we are mistaken, and especially when we do not wholly agree with what the spirit is trying to tell us, but still stay together—that is when the spirit flourishes. Then the work of the church is done because the work of the Spirit is under way.

Our loyalty then is to him who is high and lifted up, whom we worship and who calls us to a life of perfect service.

In that loyalty our common family life flourishes. We are in process of becoming—always becoming more and more—a community of trust.

Let us pray.

O God, we bring ourselves anew to thee and to thy service. Pour into our hearts such a love for thee that we may truly love our neighbors as ourselves. Fill our lives with thy motive of service and use us, Lord, use us for thine own purpose, just as thou wilt and when and where, by the power of that spirit given us through Christ, our Lord. Amen.

A Community that Cares

—⚭—

Sunday after Ascension Day,
May 23, 1971

This is the second in a series of two sermons about St. James' Church. The first last week had as its title, "A Community of Trust." The thesis was that St. James' Church is a Christian family in which its members, learning to trust one another and helped to trust one another, are helped to trust God so that they may carry out his will. We do it imperfectly but we are trying to do it. The vestry is making every effort to help us do it more perfectly. The committee structure, which it has created (referred to in your bulletin this morning), has made provision for more people to participate in the actual work, and decision making of the church and the parish meeting that it has called for this morning are two illustrations of the ways by which that "Community of Trust" is being extended.

The sermon today has to do with the purpose of our trusting one another, and in that trust, trusting God: that we may carry out his will. It has to do, therefore, with his mission; to deal with the question "What is the church for?"

St. James' Church is a "Community of Trust" in order that it may increasingly be a community that cares. That is the title of the sermon, "A Community that Cares." We trust that the world may know that God cares.

In order that we may have some sense of direction in discussing this theme, let me put it in the form of three questions: *What* is the mission of this church? *Why* is that the mission? *How* do we carry it out?

So the first question: *What* is the mission of the church? What are we here for? Its mission is what it has always been: to continue to bring into the world the new life that was first set loose by the life, death, and resurrection of Jesus and the giving of his spirit. We share that life as we share his spirit and participate in his work. That work is essentially life giving. We give his life and his spirit as we live by faith, with hope and in love and so express it that men may be given new life. This is what the church is for.

So the second question: *Why* is this the mission of the church? The only answer is because this is what God *is*. He is the spirit abroad that sets men free to live in this way, to live with confidence, to live with infinite hope for this world and for our society and with the love that can never be defeated finally, so that men may live fully as men. The crippled man is the man who lives in fear, who hasn't any hope, so has given up. God wants him to be whole.

Men are not free when they are shackled, when they are shackled by sin. Always trying to get your own way is to be shackled. We can't get our own way. When we're shackled by that kind of drive, we breed the passion that breeds war, tyranny, and oppression and fear.

Men are not free when shackled by ignorance—not able to read or write or to do sums—and so are easily exploited by other men.

Men are not free when they are shackled by poverty, and so rats share their bedrooms. Shackled because they can't get a job. Shackled by a system of welfare that destroys their spirit. Shackled by drugs because life is unbearable. Shackled by racism—never able to get ahead because of the color of one's skin.

Shackled by affluence, by possessions, unable to move as a free spirit because one is burdened with the things he possesses. Shackled by apathy, boredom, or loneliness. Shackled by a deep sense of alienation.

God sent his son to strike these shackles from the human race so that men might be free to live and to bring healing to the nations and reconciliation between brothers. He sent his spirit to affirm life, to give people grounds for having faith in themselves and their fellow men, reason for hope, a sense of direction and a strength to love even the unlovable.

This is the spirit that was sent. It was not sent in a disembodied fashion. The spirit is never disembodied. It was in the body of Jesus and then it was in the body of that company of people Jesus gathered around him. He trusted that little community. He trusted the untrustworthy one as well as the good ones. He sent them out on his mission: by the power of his spirit, he sent them in order that they might bring life to people. His spirit strengthened them. It always strengthens those who belong to his company. His spirit sent them, after they were strengthened. to touch other men, as they cared for them.

So when they went—and ever after when Christians have gone on a mission—they have always gone in response to God. He sent them. That is why worship is so terribly important because it is in worship that one has a sense of the vision of the beauty of God. One does not get that sense in isolation or in self-indulgence or in alienation. God is high and lifted up and in the light of that vision, men are sent to heal the broken spirits and bodies of men. It is that response to *God* that keeps the church from being only a social service agency, concerned only to serve the needs of men. The needs of men are served in response to God. When we respond to God, then we are sent to men.

Again, if you should ask, "Why is that so?" the only answer is because that is the way God is. That is in fact, therefore, the way life is. We catch little wisps of this in our experience. Those wisps are gathered up out of our personal life and our corporate life as we participate in that life of the company of God's people gathered together around his name. As we see him, know him and find ourselves more fully in him, more freely in him, then we respond. That response is being sent by him to men. It is sometimes called "the divine imperative."

So, that is the mission. That is the reason for it—always outward, always outward. Then the third question: "*How* do we go outward, how do we carry that mission out?" There are two ways.

First of all we carry it out by being loyal to the body to which we belong, which is the bearer of the spirit: that is, the church. I am now talking about the institutional church: this church set in the Diocese of New York, part of the Protestant Episcopal Church, part of the church of Christ, that is the church to which we belong. It is not the whole church but it is the one given us. If we are to be responsible to God, we can do so by being responsible members of his church.

Every activity of the human spirit, if it is to be effective, needs an institution—that is a structure with a backbone and with muscles and a heart and blood to carry that spirit. No idea carries power in the abstract. Love is institutionalized in marriage; learning is institutionalized in school; patriotism is institutionalized in the government; the worship of God is institutionalized in a church.

The church is God's institution as it is the bearer of his spirit. It does not own his spirit. It does not encompass all of that spirit. But insofar as it is a company of men and women where he is acknowledged as supreme, where prayers are said, where bread is broken and where there is fellowship and teaching in accord with the spirit of the earliest company, that is where the spirit is borne.

Loyalty to him, therefore, means loyalty to his institution, and disloyalty to the institution in some measure means disloyalty to him. Within the church institution we are given perfectly open, democratic procedures to change programs and to change our representatives. To separate ourselves because of disagreement with programs and representatives is to destroy the spirit. A dismembered body cannot carry a power to bring life to a broken world. It has to be as whole as possible.

The Diocese of New York does not pay its full quota to the national church, not because it is not able to, but because it does not want to. Some parishes do not contribute to the diocese or the national church, not because they are unable, but because they are unwilling. It is hard to see how this is a constructive contribution to the life of the church and to the gospel of Christ.

This parish has an unbroken tradition of responding to the request that comes from the national and diocesan church wholeheartedly as the first priority on its giving. This seems so obvious a first responsibility that it should hardly be mentioned. But it at least provides a reminder to us that our response to God begins with our response to his church.

That is one way we respond to God. The other way is our response simply to the needs of men: their physical needs, intellectual needs, spiritual needs, human needs; to respond to meet those needs as intelligently as we can. We love God as we love our neighbors as ourselves.

Our neighbor is our brother in need. The teenage addict in Yorkville, the children in the Study Club in Harlem, the displaced persons along the Jordan River, the homeless in Pakistan, the Jews in Soviet Russia, the policemen shot in the back, the emotionally overwrought around the corner, the hungry across the world, the lonely, elderly in rooming houses alone at home, and the refugees on the Indian border; all who march up and down Fifth Avenue in those parades, all who march all over Southeast Asia.

Where is our neighbor? Here—there—everywhere. Who is he? Everyman. Everyman in need.

Out of those billions scattered over the face of the globe we select a few whom we shall love as much as we love ourselves, as we give of ourselves in our time, in our talents and our energy, and of our money.

Ideally, for every dollar we spend on ourselves, we spend another dollar for our neighbor, if we are to love our neighbor as ourselves.

We love ourselves in fact a little bit more than we love our neighbors, if this is an adequate criterion to use. Last year we loved ourselves three times as much. For every three dollars we spent on ourselves, we spent one dollar on our neighbor. This year for every three dollars we spend on ourselves, we are spending two dollars on our neighbors. The direction is exactly the right direction. Next year perhaps for every three dollars we spend on ourselves we shall spend three dollars on our neighbors.

Today is something of a minor historic day in the life of this parish. Responsibility, if the by-laws suggested are adopted, will be shared by an increasing number of people and the possibility of more effective response to the mission of the church to God greatly enlarged. The area of trust will move from the vestry to the parish.

With such faith the potential for hope and love is indescribable: this trusting community expressing its caring. We can hopefully look to the future of this company of people on Madison Avenue and Seventy-First Street, gathered together to worship God, to thank him, and in his presence to catch a glimpse of his holiness and a vision of a fairer land and city and world. Then may those who gather here be happy to be sent.

So a coming in and a going out—that is the church. A coming together trusting, and a going out caring. Coming to break bread—going to give the bread of life. Coming to give thanks—going to give hope. A coming and a going in faith, hope, and love—new life—new life for men.

A trusting community that cares—so may we be. Amen.

Give us, Almighty God, we beseech thee, by the gift of thy spirit such a vision of thy holiness, and of the good that may be in us, that in the company of thy Son, and in the company of his companions, the life of this parish may go on from strength to strength and continue to find its place and meaning in thy heavenly kingdom; through Christ Our Lord. Amen.

Attica:*
Perspective and Prayer

—∞—

Sunday, September 19, 1971

I am sure that all who worship here this morning share the sense of shock at the tragic sequence of events at Attica this week. As citizens most of us no doubt agree with the editorial in *The New York Times* on the day after the rebellion was broken. It concludes with these words:

> Out of yesterday's holocaust must come a recognition that the nation has been living on borrowed time in its failure to correct the abysmal conditions that make life intolerable in Attica and virtually every other penal institution. It is as unfair to correctional officers as it is to prisoners to have such conditions continue.
>
> The state has a duty to implement swiftly the concessions it has already pledged at Attica and to move forward to more fundamental reforms. Only two weeks ago a state legislative committee found the penal system in such disarray that even to apply the term 'correction' to it bordered on the ludicrous. Prophetically, it warned that nothing basic had changed in the 'archaic conditions' that had touched off a violent one-day prisoner takeover at another state prison last November. Unless change came soon, the committee said, that earlier disturbance would merely be a 'prelude to a nightmare.'
>
> Now that the nightmare has occurred, the answer must not be more repression and increasingly bloody nightmares but thoroughgoing reform.

---

*On September 9–13, 1971, approximately 1,000 inmates at the New York state correctional facility at Attica rioted and took hostages. After negotiations stalemated, state police were ordered to re-take the prison by force, resulting in thirty-nine deaths, including ten officers and civilian employees.

As citizens we can share this common concern and a common determination to help our society bring about a "thoroughgoing reform" in our penal system.

Is there anything further that citizens who are Christians can bring? What can we who belong to Christ's Body—the church—bring in addition to concern and a will to make reform possible? This sermon is addressed to these questions.

There are, I believe, two things Christians can bring as they listen to the Word of God.

One is *perspective*. I am thinking not so much of historical perspective though it is not amiss to compare our penal system—with reforms long overdue—with the penal system of England, let us say, of the eighteenth century and observe that some progress has been made in how the law treats human begins who have broken the law.

I am rather thinking of an *eternal* perspective that Christians are able to bring to any historical period and to the events that take place within it. To have an eternal perspective is to be concerned with the *ultimate* meaning of an event in *personal* terms. The events that mean anything to you personally mean something (perhaps everything) to God.

Your happiness or sorrow, your birth or death, the birth or death of your loved ones have a meaning more than simply your personal one. They mean something to God—everything.

Likewise, the prosperity or decline of a nation, its birth or death have a meaning more than simply a national one. They also mean something to God—everything. The events in the life of a nation are more than simple historical events described in history books. This meaning is also God's meaning—ultimate, final, eternal.

This combination of ultimate and personal is set forth in the Bible lessons. Moses says in Deuteronomy 5 [paraphrasing]: "You Jews, led out of prison in Egypt and poverty, were led by God. It was God's deliverance. It was God's doing. I helped but the reason you were delivered was because God made it possible. He decided it. He chose you. And whatever you do in your actions makes all the difference in the world to him because you are his. You belong to him. Since you belong to him, act in accordance with his laws—the Ten Commandments. That is how you live. Act justly to people and you will flourish. Act unjustly and you will have a riot on your hands and your nation will die. That is [the] meaning of your history. That is its ultimate meaning—God's meaning."

The Christian understanding of the meaning of historical events is exactly the same as this Jewish understanding of ultimate meaning—with this addition: It is made personal. It is not only national, corporate, but it is also personal.

Jesus is talking in the New Testament lesson Matthew 25 about behavior and says the important thing is its meaning. What does it mean, for example, to care? To care is to care for God. It is, in a sense, to "take care" of God. You help somebody, you help God. It is you personally, dealing with God personally.

So he says [paraphrasing]: "When you give a hungry man food, you give it to me. When you give a thirsty child a cup of water, you give it to me. When you take a stranger in, you take me. You clothed a naked man, you clothed me. When you visited a sick person, you visited me. When you came to a person in prison, you came to me. When you care about prisoners, you care about me."

It is as personal as you can get: your neighbor, every neighbor in every community, every person in need, is in Christ, and you personally are in him.

So the Christian can bring some perspective. Whether it is Attica or Vietnam, the birth of your child or his death, the burst of your love or outburst of your hate—it all has ultimate meaning to God—and therefore every act of your neighbor, or your society, has some personal meaning to you.

With some kind of perspective like this then we can take our share of the blame for Attica. We don't point our finger and say: "It's the governor's fault. It's Oswald's* fault. It's the blacks' fault. It's the revolutionaries' fault."

It's all our fault—in varying degrees—but most of all, our fault when we say it's not our fault, it's not our business.

A Christian perspective then brings some sense of our common brotherhood under God and our common responsibility for our common life as a nation under God.

A Christian perspective brings also a sense that we can do something about it. That is, we can do something about living responsibly under God where we are. Everybody can't reform prisons, but everybody can reform himself. Everybody can begin again where he is to live his life

---

*Russell G. Oswald, correctional services commissioner at the time.

with integrity, begin again to care for people he has cast out of his life, be generous to those who are less fortunate—the powerless out of prison or in. Whom do you know who is rejected, despised, weak? There is Christ. You can do something to care for him.

A perspective, an eternal perspective—God's perspective upon your life as a citizen in personal terms, then, brings hope. A Christian always has hope. He never gives up. He never gives way to despair. He never cops out and says, "The hell with it."

To do that is to go to hell. Jesus' words were: those people go to "everlasting damnation." That kind of damnation is already here for those who have rejected everything, who no longer care. It is not otherworldly; it is now. They already are in hell—solitary confinement.

But those others who keep on, who continue to care, who keep on steadily working with integrity where they are, in touch with Jesus where they are, for them he says they go into "eternal life." And that eternal life likewise begins now for all who continue to care. That is, they go on here and now with hope—and therefore with a sense of purpose and a zest for living—they are carried by hope because they know they are God's and therefore live with infinite hope.

At the outset, I said that Christians can bring two things to our nation. One is *perspective*. That is, the perspective that comes from the ultimate being joined with the personal.

Now there is another thing that can be brought by Christian people. It has to do with how you can put things into perspective. Things fall into perspective when you pray about them. It is prayer that binds the most ultimate and the most personal together. That is how the personal relationship between God and a man develops. Without prayer the God-man relationship remains impersonal. It remains historical, theological, rational, dry, lifeless.

Now to pray is simply to offer our *personal* concerns to God, who is our ultimate concern, to ask to see them from his perspective and call upon him for his help to strengthen us as we try to live as he would have us—as citizens of this nation, and as persons who belong not only to our nation but to him.

So—let us pray.

God, our Father, we lay before you now our common concern that rises from our responsibilities as citizens of this nation and especially from the prison in Attica.

We ask you to comfort and strengthen all those involved in this tragedy that they may know that in each one thy Son dwells, that in their pain he suffers, in their reconciliation he is reconciled, and that in him lies their hope.

We pray for: all those in that prison; those who put them there; those who guard them; those transferred and their guards.

We pray for: the men killed—prisoners and hostages; those who killed them; their families and loved ones; all who mourn.

We pray for: the governor of this state; Mr. Oswald; those who enforce the law; all who bear the responsibility to govern—that in their decisions they may wait upon you to be guided by your wisdom and saved from false choices.

We pray for: this nation; this state; this city; for those who live with us, all men of every color of whatever creed—and especially for the hungry, the thirsty, the strangers, the naked, the sick, the prisoners in whom thy Son dwells and in whose name we pray, Our Savior Jesus Christ. Amen.

What St. James' Church Is Up To

—m—

Sunday, November 21, 1971

On the scaffolding on the building adjacent to the church on the north—the building which Mr. Michel has just referred to as purchased by this church this past year to provide a center for community work and outreach beyond the church—on this scaffolding there is a sign which reads, "Polishing not Demolishing." That immortal phrase was coined, I think, by [Mrs. Moldovsky, the parish assistant]. Its purpose is to let the public know what St. James' Church is up to next door—polishing not demolishing. Well, this sermon is about that process; to comment on what St. James' Church is up to not only next door, but here, in this building, in its total program, symbolized by the budget presented today. It is in part in response to requests for amplification of remarks made at the rector's council last week.

Therefore the sermon has to do with the spirit entering the material, the spirit entering human life, the spirit entering bricks and mortar, the spirit entering Madison Avenue. It is illustrated by a poem and by the life of the man who wrote that poem, Robert Frost. The poem is an introduction to his collected poems, *In the Clearing,* and it begins like this:

> But God's own descent
> Into flesh was meant
> As a demonstration
> That the supreme merit
> Lay in risking spirit
> In substantiation.
>
> (From "Kitty Hawk," *In the Clearing,* 1975)

Risking spirit in substance. Risking spirit to the ways of willful men. Risking spirit to building. Risking spirit to money. Risking spirit to St. James' Church.

The spirit can never be controlled. That's why it is so risky to trust. It can never be captured. It can never be structured. Once you believe you have grasped it, it flies away. Once you believe you know how to call it, take advantage of it, put yourself in it, the structures are destroyed.

In the latter years of his life, Robert Frost used to spend a month a year at Amherst College making himself available to talk with students, faculty, and members of the town where he had lived earlier in his life. One evening in a fraternity house a student asked him, "Mr. Frost, what is the best course of study to take in order to get the best education at Amherst College?" He replied, "Oh, it doesn't make any difference. Take anything you want to. After a while you catch on, or you don't. You can't do anything except hang around. Take what you want to take until the spirit touches you."

One thing St. James' Church is about is to make it possible for people to hang around until they catch on; to do anything they want to do, in their terms, around their interests, until the spirit touches them, or doesn't touch them. Some people like to tutor in a study club in East Harlem; others like to meet on Thursdays to pray. Some like to work in the church school; others are more concerned about community activities. Some like to wash dishes (at least prepare the dishes for washing); others like to take up the offering. Some like to chaperon teenage dances (not enough!); others like to dance. It doesn't make any difference what you do. After a while you catch on, or you don't.

One man caught on in this way. He wanted to teach Sunday school. He thought it would be fine to teach the substance of the Christian faith to young boys, so he took a class. He had a very difficult time with eleven- and twelve-year-old boys. This year he said, "I'm going to forget all that stuff. I am just going to let those kids know that I care for them." The class came alive and he says, "It is exciting!" Substance arose out of the spirit. He caught on. He risked the spirit and the spirit transformed "the stuff" of the Christian gospel into a living reality for young boys. That's catching on!

> But God's own descent
> Into flesh was meant
> As a demonstration

That the supreme merit
Lay in risking spirit
In substantiation.

That is one thing the church is about—risking spirit, making it possible for people on their terms, on the basis of their interests to catch on, to create structures so that the spirit may touch them when the time is right.

If this is for St. James' people, the second thing the church is about is for Madison Avenue people—people who will never be inside this church but walk up and down in front of it every day. The spirit which touches people inside is meant to be expressed to those people outside.

The poem goes on like this:

Spirit enters flesh
And for all it's worth
Charges into earth
In birth after birth
Ever fresh, ever fresh.

That is the spirit. It is never old, always new, always exciting, always creating. The spirit possesses and moves and empowers people for their lives.

One of the former presidents of Amherst College once approached Robert Frost and asked if he might have his permission to use his name to establish a chair for a visiting professor of poetry. Mr. Frost replied, "Why, yes, of course. I should be honored to have you use my name." So the President went about fund-raising. He came back after some months and said, "Mr. Frost, I have been asked the question, and I have to find the answer to this question: What is the visiting professor of poetry going to do?" "Do?" he replied, "Why he's not going to do anything. He is just supposed to *be*. He is to be a poet. He is to hang around Amherst College and listen to his muse, to respond to that muse as he is moved to; to let students know that there is a muse abroad in the world. They had better listen for the voice of their muse if they are going to live. He is to help them discern that voice that's speaking to them, their own muse. You can't write a job description for a poet. He's just meant to *be*." The President looked at him. He did not raise any money, and the chair was not founded.

The church is just meant to *be*. On this block between Seventy-First and Seventy-Second Streets. It's meant to be a Christian presence, a reminder that there is a muse abroad in the world; and to testify to the spirit of that muse that all men may be reminded to search for and heed their own; to be reminded that they can be fully themselves when they are filled with the right spirit.

> Spirit enters flesh
> And for all it's worth
> Charges into earth
> In birth after birth
> Ever fresh, ever fresh.

The renewal of men's spirits by the spirit, ever fresh, ever fresh. Generation after generation, birth after birth, people walking by, reminded of that spirit by a Christian presence, the visible presence of that spirit here.

That is what the church is about, a city block where there is response to a spirit within and response to the same spirit without, a city block committed to the welfare of people that they may be strengthened in the spirit. St. James' Church, no matter how much money it raises and gives away, will never transform the city of New York. But it can help the spirit transform people and they can transform the city.

The closing lines of this poem are these:

> We may take the view
> That its derring-do
> Thought of in the large
> Is one mighty charge
> On our human part
> Of the soul's ethereal
> Into the material.

One mighty charge—one deep conviction—one fundamental commitment—one pledge of loyalty—one gift that costs—

> On our human part
> Of the soul's ethereal
> Into the material.

So the work of God done as the work of this church is done. This is how God's own descent into the flesh was meant. Amen.

Your Journey with
the Wise Men

—⚏—

The First Sunday after Epiphany,
January 9, 1972

Now when Jesus was born in Bethlehem of Judea in the days of Herod the king, behold, wise men from the East came to Jerusalem saying, "Where is he who has been born king of the Jews? For we have seen his star in the East and have come to worship him." When they had heard the king they went their way; and lo, the star, which they had seen in the East went before them, till it came to rest over the place where the child was. When they saw the star, they rejoiced exceedingly with great joy; and going into the house they saw the child with Mary his mother, and they fell down and worshipped him. Then opening their treasures, they offered him gifts—gold and frankincense and myrrh. (Mt. 2:1–2, 9–11, RSV)

That is the text. The title of the sermon is "Your Journey with the Wise Men." The wise men were probably astrologers from Babylonia. The science of the day was the study of the stars. The scientists were the astrologers, the mathematicians, the navigators.

Those three wise men had come on a journey of several days from the East to the West. They had gone over the desert, through the desolate landscape, through forlorn little villages, deserted remote little towns. They had gone in the cold mid-winter, beset by brigands, threatened by storm.

What that journey was like has tantalized the imagination of Christian men and women over the centuries. Since the first century, men and women have tried to put themselves in the place of those wise men and to identify, insofar as they could, their following of the star.

In the most glorious period of the flowering of Anglicanism in the first part of the seventeenth century, there was an extraordinary group of divines of the post-Elizabethan settlement who charted the course that Anglicanism has followed since then, primarily with regard to the place of "the gentle art of reason"–the following of truth. One outstanding leader was Bishop Lancelot Andrewes. He tried to identify himself with the wise men in a sermon that he preached for King James I on Christmas Day 1622. He is describing the journey: "A cold coming they had of it at that time of the year, just the worst time of the year to take a journey and especially a long journey. The ways deep, the weather sharp, the days short, the sun farthest off, 'the very dead of winter.'"

Three hundred years later in the early part of this century, T. S. Eliot begins his poem "The Journey of the Magi" with those words of Lancelot Andrewes. Let me read them to you:

> A cold coming we had of it,
> Just the worst time of the year
> For a journey, and such a long journey:
> The ways deep and the weather sharp,
> 'The very dead of winter.'
> And the camels galled, sore-footed, refractory,
> Lying down in the melting snow.
> There were times we regretted
> The summer palaces on slopes, the terraces,
> And the silken girls bringing sherbet.
> Then the camel men cursing and grumbling
> And running away, and wanting their liquor and women,
> And the night-fires going out, and the lack of shelters,
> And the cities hostile and the towns unfriendly
> And the villages dirty and charging high prices:
> A hard time we had of it.
> At the end we preferred to travel all night,
> Sleeping in snatches,
> With the voices singing in our ears, saying
> That this was all folly.

Anyone who has ever followed a star, his own star, has had a hard time of it on his journey. There is no journey a man undertakes with a purpose, setting a direction, seeking a goal, searching for a journey's end, no such journey that does not have hard times. If you have a star, count on hard times.

All people who have ever had a vision, who have ever wanted their lives to count for something more than the general run, have always heard voices singing in their ears saying that "this was all folly." If you have seen your star and are on a journey following it, you won't ever be surprised at the hard times, nor at the voices saying that all you are doing is sheer folly. Nor, if you are wise, will you pay any attention to them. Hard times, jibes of foolishness are to be expected.

The wise man, into whose mouth Eliot puts his words, continues his description with this verse:

> Then at dawn we came down to a temperate valley.
> Wet, below the snow line, smelling of vegetation;
> With a running stream and a water-mill beating
> the darkness,
> And three trees on the low sky,
> And an old white horse galloped away in the meadow.
> Then we came to a tavern with vine-leaves over the
> lintel,
> Six hands at an open door dicing for pieces of silver,
> And feet kicking the empty wine-skins.
> But there was no information, and so we continued
> And arrived at evening, not a moment too soon
> Finding the place; it was (you may say) satisfactory.

If you have ever followed your own star, on your own journey, you have always watched the games that people play, the drinks that people drink, the lives that people lead. On our journey we are drawn—we are tempted to be drawn—to play those games, to drink those drinks, to lead those lives as though those games and those drinks and those lives were better than our journey—the hardness of it, the foolishness of it. We ask the players and the drinkers about the road, but there is no information." ". . . there was no information, and so we continued. . . ." The continuing when there is no information, the going ahead when there is no way except in the dark, when the star's light that shone so brilliantly at the outset is engulfed by the clouds' blackness, and we wonder if there ever had been a star.

The everlasting going ahead when the shadows fall and the failures begin; when all partings with companions along the way seem final; when the burdens are too great, it seems, to be borne, and the vision long since dimmed is extinguished.

". . . and so we continued and arrived at evening, not a moment too soon finding the place; it was (you may say) satisfactory." When you persevere, when you find the place, when your heart's desire is won, there may be no great exultation, no deep sense of absolute fulfillment; the goal quite different from your expectation—perhaps just the opposite but ". . . (you may say) satisfactory."

The satisfactions are quite simply in continuing and in the evening "finding the place." Not the place you expected at all, but a different place. Not the people you had anticipated, but people who have changed. Not the end of the journey at the end of your road, but a different journey's end.

No high position ever attained but perhaps bedrock integrity discovered. No prestige and honor given but a quiet, gentle grace and satisfaction. No riches in your home but faithfulness. No great authority to change anybody's life and direct anybody's destiny but peace in your heart to live with.

So the wise man concludes:

> All this was a long time ago, I remember,
> And I would do it again, but set down
> This set down
> This: were we led all that way for
> Birth or Death? There was a Birth, certainly,
> We had evidence and no doubt. I had seen birth
> and death,
> But had thought they were different; this birth was
> Hard and bitter agony for us, like Death, our death.
> We returned to our places, these Kingdoms,
> But no longer at ease here, in the old dispensation,
> With an alien people clutching their gods.
> I should be glad of another death.

Once you have seen a star and followed it—once you have endured hard times and resisted the foolishness of it—once you have persevered to the end—once you have had a vision and obeyed it—the old life is never the same again. The same old habits have lost their control. Once you have had a vision of what your life might be and have been loyal to that vision, the flat humdrum of routine of nothing ahead, of no place to go, of nothing any more but games and drinks and the same old merry-go-round, you are no longer at ease with an "alien people," playing games with one another.

"I should be glad of another death." To be dead to all that which is old is to be glad in a new birth. To be dead to the "dead-ended-ness" of life, to the sense of nothingness, to the bitterness and cynicism and the emptiness, to the standing pat, to the fear of ever taking a journey, of ever breaking out, of ever going on following a bright star, obeying a higher vision. To be dead to all that which is in the past is to be glad of another death and to welcome the birth of a new life. This is to welcome the birth of the Christ Child in Bethlehem.

So search for your star. Follow it. What is that vision of your life that you are called to follow and to obey?

You cannot follow your star because you cannot find it? You don't know? If you cannot follow and find your star, you can find *him*. You can begin before him. Come to worship him. That is what the journey is all about.

Make your offerings to him—your gold, frankincense, and myrrh. Make the offering of the best you know, of your will, of your heart's desire. Give him some of your substance. Make an offering that costs something. Give him the best you've got, your best intention for your best life right now—even if it's dark.

Make that offering to him in the dark. Then look up. *There* is your star. Follow it.

Good journey. Amen.

The Making of Christ—
Mark of Maturity

—◦◦◦—

The Second Sunday after Epiphany,
January 16, 1972

"The Making of Christ—Mark of Maturity:" that is the title of this sermon. The theme is "Christian growth." . . . [Editor's note: A detailed description of the parish's education program has been omitted from this version.] . . . the purpose of Christian education is to help young people and adults come to a deeper and deeper understanding of the Christian story and to help them demonstrate for themselves, in their own lives, its truth. Any church which does not take education seriously is no church. The central question that any thinking man asks of the Christian faith is: "If it is true, how do I find out?"

The answer, of course, is you find out only as you live it, or more accurately, as you try to live it. It's a living truth; it's not a propositional truth. So this month two confirmation classes meeting regularly to ask: "What is the Christian story? Is it true?" The answers will be different for fourteen-year-olds and forty-year-olds. Adolescents and the generation that their parents represent do not have the same understanding of what is real or what values are worthwhile, or indeed whether facts and values are related. They do not have the same understanding of the truth.

Nor probably do you who are here this morning. It is unlikely that any three people here would have exactly the same understanding of what the Christian story is and what it means, or the same understanding of how true it might be. Most of you completed your formal Christian education—at least in the classroom academic sense—with the last course you took in religion at college or in school, or perhaps even in confirmation class. That kind of learning came to an end a little while ago.

What hasn't come to an end is your living. You have had to go on making decisions and every decision you have made in your life has had something to do with values that you felt were important. You decided to marry one person and not another, which is to say, that she or he was more valuable for you than the other person. Or, you decided not to marry anybody; that is, that condition was worth more for you. You decided to take one job rather than another job, or you changed jobs, because the values by which you live caused you to do so.

You have had to make some sense out of life. If you have been involved in it, you have been hurt by it. If you have loved anybody, for example, you have known ecstasy, but you have also known the pain of love. If you have lifted your eyes and observed the human race, you have seen something of the glory of man; and if you have lowered your eyes, you have seen how depraved he can be. If you have looked within, you have seen in yourself something of the glory and something of the depravity.

To find some meaning, to make some sense out of living, is probably one of the reasons you are here in church. You try to find, either once again or for the first time, some sense to the enterprise of living; to see if it is possible to sense the presence of Someone or Something beyond the routine and the human. You search for some guidelines of values for life. As you are reminded of God and his values and come to worship him in spirit and in truth—at least in as good spirit and with as much truth as you can muster—you may in fact be helped to find some direction for living. You may be given some surge of strength that enables you to get over the next hurdle, and to continue to grow in the knowledge and love of God in ways that are most appropriate for your life.

So Christian education has been going on all your life long—Christian education in its essentials—as you continue to mature in understanding and, hopefully, as you grow not only in age but in grace. You grow from a sense of *feeling* secure as in the Primary Department, in God's presence (hopefully never losing that sense), into a more *reasoned* and rational faith which an intelligent man can believe, in order to make sense out of his experience and so *live* by it in all the decisions that he makes. While there may be wide differences among you about how you interpret the Christian faith, and indeed in how you live it, growth in maturity follows very much the same pattern. So we come to the marks of the mature man—the mature man in Christ.

The first mark is *personal.* Your grandparents or your parents might say, "I believe in a personal God, who is personally concerned about me, with what is best for me, and he will help me as I trust him." Your children probably would not use that language. They might say, "I have to figure out where my head is at." God in personal terms is knowing where your head is at. Where is your head? Do you know? That's where God is. Your personal God. Listen to him—there.

This sense of a personal relationship—your own inner, unique self in its most intimate way related to a personal God who is the most ultimate value in the universe—this sense of a personal relationship is the most steadying and the most exalting experience there is in life. It is the only way one can stay grounded, rooted, and continue to keep in touch with where his head is. And at the same time, it is the most exalting experience that there is.

Emily Dickinson describes exaltation:

> . . . the going of an inland soul to sea,
> Past the houses—past the headlands—
> Into deep Eternity.
>> (From "Exultation is the Going")

That sense of being carried, of moving, of adventure, of being courageous and unafraid and letting the tides and the winds take one into eternity—that is a personal mark of a mature man of faith.

The second mark is *communal,* that is, we are our brothers' keepers. Eliot's question was, "What life have we if we have not life together?" And the answer is—none! We meet God as we meet our neighbor. This does not mean our Episcopal neighbor (though it does mean that—and that may be the most difficult brotherhood to establish). It means our Jewish brothers, our Roman Catholic brothers, our Puerto Rican brothers, our jailbird brothers, our dope addict brothers, our AWOL brothers, and our General brothers. It means all brothers in every society, on every level, not just our kind—perhaps especially not our kind.

When we identify the second mark—this communal mark—we are saying that the God who cares for us personally in our lives, and in this church, is the God who cares personally for everybody in every church, in every synagogue, and in no church and no temple—all men. What we want for them is what we want for ourselves—that sense of security—of knowing that we are at home in the universe and that we are moving toward truth which is revealed more and more.

This is described by a Roman Catholic scholar pointing out why the church is concerned about the social as well as the personal element in religion. John Courtney Murray writes, "What the church ultimately wants in the temporal order is to see there reflected, in civic friendship, the spirit of love that is the primary expression of her faith. She wants this for the sake of the city, as essential to its own good; she wants it too as the necessary expression of her own faith . . . love of the city's common good . . . is itself . . . a form of the love of the true God . . ."*

Now since there is no such thing as instant knowledge of God, and there is no such thing as instant brotherhood of men, the third mark of Christian maturity is simply *staying* in the Presence, staying with the questions; staying and coming back, staying in Christ and coming back to him; letting *him* be the mark. Letting *him* take the action. Letting *him* do the work. Letting *him* do the leading and the drawing and the growing. It is being willing to have *him* grow in you.

The author of the letter to the Ephesians puts it this way. He is talking about maturity ". . . speaking the truth in love, we are to grow up in every way into him who is the head, into Christ from whom the whole body upbuilds itself in love." We are to grow up into *him* . . . We cannot, by taking thought, add an inch to our stature. We cannot grow ourselves. We can, however, permit Christ to grow in us.

So we conclude—there is that *primary department* and the sense of God's eternal love and care. We are, therefore, never to be afraid and never to give up. There is that sense of security and as we mature we find that our security and peace are in *him,* not in our feelings about him.

There are the *confirmation classes* and the conviction that we are never to grow out of those questions about the truth of the Christian faith. As we mature, we find deeper and deeper understandings of what it is.

There is the *living*—we never outgrow making decisions for living increasingly, hopefully in love. As we mature, we become more and more unafraid to speak the truth in love.

In a word, when we grow up, we grow up into *him.* He made us in order that we might make him.

---

*John Courtney Murray, S.J., "The Roman Catholic Church," http://woodstock .georgetown.edu/library/Murray/1948g%20.htm

The making of Christ—the mark of maturity.

Let us pray:

O eternal God, you have set within us a spirit which answers your spirit. Give us the faith to follow that spirit in the person of Jesus who keeps that spirit so obviously before us. Teach us to be led by him in pursuit of you until we find and let the whole world feel and see that things which were cast down are being raised up; and things which are grown old are being made new, as by you in us Christ is made and renewed this day and always. Amen.

A Life to Live—A Way to Pray:
The Quest For Identity

—∞—

The First Sunday in Lent,
February 20, 1972

We have begun this Lent a series of sermons entitled *A Life to Live— A Way to Pray*. Their intent is to help us relate our living and our praying so we can bring the living and the praying closer together and, perhaps, at certain crucial points in our life have the living and praying identical—that is, our most personal, intimate living part and parcel of our ultimate destiny.

For the living side of this series, we shall consider the issues that seem uppermost in the minds of people in our day. What are the issues you have to face simply because you are a human being at the end of the twentieth century? And for our praying, as a guide we shall take the Lord's Prayer. How does our living—the things we are most concerned about in life—fit into our praying? How does our praying fit into our living? How can our life and the Lord's Prayer be one?

Perhaps the first, perhaps the underlying question that goes on all our days, perhaps the issue that remains with us until the day we die is the question of trying to find out who, precisely, we are. The first words in the Lord's Prayer are "Our father." Perhaps we can know who we are only when we know who our father is, when we know whom we address when we pray. So the title of the sermon is "The Quest for Identity." This search begins when we are first conscious of ourselves in relationship to other people—first of all our mother—and it goes on until the day we die, unless somewhere along the line we give up and no longer struggle to find out who we are on deeper and deeper levels of understanding.

I suppose that when most of us begin to pray, we have a very unclear idea of whom we are addressing or what we are addressing. We need help for living. That is the origin of most prayer. So we turn in faith and hope to a power or a force that is, we trust, greater and better than we are, and in some measure of faith and with some hope, we ask for help. Jesus said, when you pray to that power, the way to address him is by saying "Our father."

Some people today would say that the way to address that power is to say "Our mother." An article in the magazine section of the *The New York Times* last Sunday, dealing with the liberation movement of women and male chauvinism, gave a new translation to that text from Genesis which describes the act of creation, "And God created man in his own image," by translating it, "And God created woman in her own image."* (And there was appropriate visual representation: a new version of Michelangelo's painting in the Sistine Chapel.) You will recall Miss [Emmeline] Pankhurst's comment in another generation to her fellow suffragettes who were facing arrest when she said, "Do not fear. Trust God. She will protect you."

I use these illustrations not to make fun of the women's liberation movement—there is too much truth in what they say for that, and furthermore, on the test that was given in that article, I did very poorly. (It is called "The Male Chauvinist Pig Test.")—but rather for two other reasons, the first rather obvious and the other perhaps a little more subtle.

The first reason is that obviously the characteristics of a father, alone, are not adequate to describe the characteristics of God. They can point to one side of God's nature, but only one side; that side that represents power, authority, force, command, laying down the law, judgment, discipline, wisdom. These are all characteristics of what we call a "father figure." It is a very natural figure to use, a very natural symbol of God in a patriarchal society.

But the "father figure" needs a "mother figure" in order to do justice to all of the characteristics, or a wider cross section of the characteristics of God who is the creator of all life. The "father figure" needs a "mother figure" just for the act of creation itself. Both are required. The feminine qualities are as necessary for the whole living of human beings as the

---

*Kathleen Neuer, "Happy St. Valentine's Day! The Male Chauvinist Pig Test," *New York Times Magazine,* February 13, 1972, Page SM21.

masculine—the comforting, the assuring, the accepting, the nursing, the feeding, the emotional, the feeling, the sensitive, the intuitive, the holding, the grounding, the reassuring, the rooting in nature. All of these characteristics—both feminine and masculine—are essential in some measure and in different proportions for every human being, and they are together necessary to point to that wholeness in the ultimate reality of God. God is *all* life and more. So when we call upon him, we are calling upon a power who encompasses all of what we know of as reality borne in the earliest instance by fathers and mothers, and of course infinitely more than that.

That is the first reason: real life is made up of fathers and their authority and power, and of mothers and their comfort and feeling, to take but two typical qualities for each. The second reason why father and mother relationships are necessary for our thinking of God—and by extension, the relationships that we have with brothers and sisters, and uncles and aunts, and grandparents, and later the relationships between husbands and wives and parents and children—indeed the totality of this fabric of personal family relationships—is that we know God first and foremost, and forever, primarily within flesh and blood relationships.

We come into life born of a man and a woman creating us, who care for us and dominate us, who discipline us and love us, who frighten us when they are angry and who kiss us when they are sorry, who terrify us when we are naughty and who forgive us when they are gracious. And our response is very similar: a mixture of loving and of hating; of wanting always to be safe at home and of needing to strike out from home (a need sometimes to strike out from home made possible only by striking back at home); our accepting them and always being fearful of losing them; our rejecting them and being terrified at the thought of their death; our wanting them to die and knowing that parents can never die. All these blood, family, personal relationships—competitive, supporting, rivalries, loves, friends, enemies—all these relationships help determine who we are. We are formed to become who we are through these fundamental, very personal, very human, flesh and blood relationships.

So, when we turn to God and say "you," we cannot turn to him except out of these relationships, these and more. We pray to God out of anger when a father has dominated us: "O God, my father never has liked me. He doesn't like me now; he never will like me. You help me." We pray out of a broken heart when a loved one dies: "O God, help us, help him." We pray out of anguish when we don't know how to express our personal loyalties: "O God, what shall we do?" We pray out of a full heart when a child is born: "O God, thank you." We pray out of guilt when we sin: "O God, I am sorry. Forgive me." We pray out of perplexity when we must make decisions: "O God, how can I choose the best and count for the most?"

Well, you see the point. It is from within the process and the pressures of living that prayer rises. It is through the pressures of living that God presses. It is through the living of all these characteristics of life that you first came to know and touch in those close personal relationships—through your parents, and brothers and sisters, and husbands and wives and children—that your prayer begins to move out of your living.

How do you respond to authority? How do you exercise authority? Who makes up the rules of your life? Do you make them up? Are they imposed on you by somebody else? Do you impose your rules on your children, on your wife? Do you obey those rules yourself?

Whom do you comfort? Who comforts you? Who is there to pick you up when you fall down? Who do you pick up because you are standing by and are there when you are needed? To whom are you loyal? Why? Who is loyal to you?—because of your command, or because of their love, or because they are caught? What are you both fascinated by, yet fear, at the same time?—birth? death? sex? What is there in your life that makes your life unbearable, and yet you must bear it because you want to bear it? What are the relationships in your life that make no sense, that have lost all meaning? Why? Where is the conflict in your life that must be solved, and you can't solve it and you know nobody else is going to solve it? Will you face it or repress it? What will you do?

Where, in a word, are the pressures of living forcing you beyond yourself? That is where God is pressing, the One to whom, when you pray, you say, "Our father, *you.*" Pray through those living pressures to your father, because that is where he is.

As you come through your living and praying to know more and more who he is and how he is shaping your life, you come to know more and more who you are—*his.* As you go through life, as you go through life praying, you come to say, "I know who I am, because I know who he is, and that I am his. I have been through enough to come to know in part who I am, and I will stake my life on it. And with God's help, will continue in that knowledge; that knowledge and love of myself, and of him, and of my neighbors, my brothers and sisters; all those personal relationships."

So when you pray, through the pressure points of life, to both the authority and the comfort, the power and the feeling of that spirit in the universe that lies behind all that is created, say "Our father, *you*." He is a personal God to whom you pray.

This final word: When you pray, don't think you have to try to begin a relationship with God—it has already begun. You don't have to build it—he began it, he established it. He established it through your mother and your father, and your brothers and your sisters, and he continues it through every relationship you have in every aspect of your living.

He made that relationship very clear when he sent his son to come into the world that we might become his sons. Saint Paul says that we might be adopted as sons of God.

This is true, not just for Christians, but for all men—good men, evil men, men who love Christ, men who never heard of Christ, men who wonder about Christ, men who hate Christ. It is the Christians who know the relationship because they know who they are, because they know who their father is, and therefore they try to live as the sons of God, as his disciples, by living and praying together: "Our father, *you*."

Let us pray:

Our father, you made us. You made us so that we are restless until we rest in you. Accept, we beseech you, those pressure points in life where we know we need you. And help us. For you are our father, and we know who we are because you sent your son, our brother, Jesus Christ. Amen.

Diocesan Mission '72

—∿—

The Seventeenth Sunday after Trinity, September 24, 1972

Yesterday (September 23rd) there was a great service in the Cathedral of St. John the Divine. Bishop Moore was installed as the successor of Bishop Donegan as diocesan bishop of the diocese. You may read about it in *The New York Times* on the front page today.

In the morning, before the installation, there was a convocation at which time the bishop presented what has come to be called Mission '72 to the parishes and the people of the diocese. It is a program to mark the beginning of his period as bishop—a program of renewal and stewardship for the entire diocese. We are to take part in that. It is a program for stewardship and renewal not only for the diocese but for the diocese in relationship to the national church and in relationship to the parishes of the Church.

Seventeen years ago when Bishop Moore was vicar at Grace Church in Jersey City and I was the dean of Trinity Cathedral in Newark, he asked me to come one day to meet with the women in his parish, to interpret the work of the cathedral—what the cathedral is, how it happened to be there, what it does, how his parish and people were involved in the life of the cathedral. He said, "Remember that they are very simple people in this parish, so please give a very simple talk."

The day before the talk was to be given, he called to make final arrangements and concluded by saying, "Don't forget to keep that talk simple." So the next afternoon I drove along that scenic highway between Newark and Jersey City, went in the Parish House and just before I was introduced, heard him say, "Remember, keep it simple."

I talked about the cathedral as the mother church of the diocese—as the old homestead. That was the original house founded by the first settlers in 1745. When the next generation came and the family began to grow and the children to leave home, they left the old homestead, went out, and established churches of their own.

Just as members of a family come back to the old homestead from time to time to celebrate great family anniversaries, so Episcopalians from all over the diocese come back from time to time on great occasions to celebrate in the cathedral, because we are all members of the same family gathered together around a bishop whose cathedral was in that old, old church. That was what made it a cathedral; that's where the bishop's chair was. So we honored him as the one around whom we gathered, and through whom we were all one, as people honored their grandparents when they go back to the old homestead.

As I sat down to something less than thunderous applause, Bishop Moore leaned over and said, "I said 'simple,' but I didn't mean *that* simple."

So I'm going to talk very simply this morning about the national church, the diocesan church, and St. James' Church. There are certain simple facts of life in the church. The first simple fact is that the Episcopal Church is a national church. We belong to the Protestant Episcopal Church *in the United States of America.* That church came into being during a national revolution. Every Anglican church is first of all a national church in communion with the Archbishop of Canterbury. That is the characteristic of Anglicanism, and it is what makes us Episcopalians. If we did not have a national church, we would not have an Episcopal Church. We could still be Christians—thank God—but we couldn't be Episcopal Christians.

The second simple fact is that the essential unit within the Episcopal Church is the diocese. The diocese is made up of lay people and clergy in relationship to a bishop who has jurisdiction over that particular area— a bishop who received his authority through a service of the national church. The diocese is made up of clergy ordained by the bishop through the authority of the national church, and lay people baptized as members of the whole church of Christ. They are not baptized into the local congregation (although many people sometimes act as though they were) or into a diocese. They are baptized into the Episcopal Church as part of the church of Christ.

And the third simple fact is that we belong together—a national church and a diocesan church. We are members one of another. We rise together in strength and when we are divided, we fall in weakness. The way to build a strong national church is to build a strong diocese. And a strong diocese means a strong national church.

We belong to the same family although we have different diocesan loyalties as well as different parish loyalties. We are who we are because of our common loyalty to the whole church. So as people in a diocese pledge loyalty to a bishop of that diocese, they also pledge their loyalty to support the church that gave him his authority, the Episcopal Church in the United States of America, and to its head, the Presiding Bishop, and to the whole Catholic church and *its* head, Jesus Christ.

A fourth simple fact. (There are going to be five.) As the diocese is the unit within the national church, so the parish is the unit within the diocese. What the diocesan national church relationship is—its interdependency— is even more true of parishes in relationship to the diocese. If there are strong parishes, there will be a strong diocese. If parishes are divided and competitive, and if they are hostile to the diocese, it will be a weak diocese.

The foundation of the diocese is built on the parishes because that is where the people of God come together to worship, where they come to know one another, and to meet one another, where they come to themselves, where they understand what the mission of the church comes to be. It is where the Gospel becomes personal in personal relationships. It is where you may understand that somebody cares for you, where you may gather together to worship, to pray, to carry on the mission of the church.

You will hear a good deal about this program of Mission '72 this fall as the diocese looks forward to its renewal and we look forward to parish renewal. We shall participate in that mission simply because we are members of this Diocesan family.

Beyond that, we shall look forward to our own renewal and the deepening of our life of worship, our caring for one another, our stewardship, and our concern for the people who do not belong to St. James' Church (and who would never darken it doors) but to whom we are bound because they are fellow human beings in need.

The last simple fact. Renewal of a national, or diocesan, or parish church rises from personal renewal. That is very simple inner renewal, inner trust, inner purpose, inner vision.

The church is a company of people, but it is people who are bound together by a certain spirit, and that spirit speaks to each of us within. It helps us ask such questions as, "When you are alone, what do you really think about? When you are alone, do you give any thought to what you are doing with your life? Do you give any thought to where you are going? Are you going in the direction you want to go? Are you becoming yourself day by day, or are you giving way to pressures so you become less and less yourself? Are you pleased with what you see happening to you?"

Such questions as these have to do with your inner integrity. How you respond to them—how you respond to life (and God)—determines what the vitality of your religious faith really is. And they are always answered inwardly first of all.

So the renewal of a parish church always rises out of personal renewal. It is people gathered together. But we are not gathering together in Central Park, we are gathering together in a church that is built that God may be worshipped. When we gather together, we look above us, and ahead of us. If you look above where you are sitting, and ahead of you, you look right at Christ. You look at the cross; you look at the place where bread is broken; you see the representation of a company of people, his disciples; and you also look within.

The one who is over the altar and who is above us, is also within us, among us in this company.

When you are silent—and maybe one of the greatest contributions of the church today is to provide a place there is some silence—when you are silent, you might ask him who is within, "Are you there? Are you really there?" Ask him that, and he may say "Yes." You may ask, "Will you help me?" He may answer, "Of course." And if you should ask "How?", he will probably say, "Look at me. Attend me. Trust me. Don't worry too much about telling me about yourself; I know. You just look and listen."

Then, if you can, do something because of that look: give an apology, write a letter, send a gift, give a thanks, make a telephone call. What is it? Do it. He says, "I do it with you." That's all the help you need for today.

That's the way you get renewed today. Renewal is a continuing process of churches, of parishes, and of people. He is the renewal. Let us pray. This prayer is the prayer for Mission '72:

Almighty God, Lord of history and our day, who has set before us the awesome vocation of opening our eyes to your glory and of carrying your love to the lives of our people, come down upon us in the power of your Spirit that we may be continually reborn in Christ. May we seek your kingdom, bring your gospel to the world, and strengthen your church in this diocese. This is our Mission for '72 and all our years. Help us in the name of our Lord and Savior, Jesus Christ. Amen.

The Knock on The Door

—⁓—

The Twenty-fourth Sunday after Trinity, November 12, 1972

The lesson that was read this morning [Luke 10:1–24]—the Commissioning of the Seventy—might be called the first Every Member Canvass. Jesus sent his disciples and the most committed of his earliest followers to go out two by two into every town and place where he himself was about to come. "I send you," he said, "as lambs in the midst of wolves. Some places will receive you and when they do you can say to them, 'The Kingdom of God is very near to you.' And peace will remain in that house.

"You will go to other places where they will not receive you. You can also say to them, 'The Kingdom of God is very near you.' But don't stay; shake the dust of that town off your feet. They will receive their due. They will receive what they wish to receive." He concluded the commissioning by saying, "He who hears you hears me. He who rejects you rejects me. And he who rejects me rejects him who sent me."

It is now nearly two thousand years later. St. James' Church is holding its first Every Member Canvass in the sense that for the first time the vestry and other committed members of the parish—in curious fact, just about seventy of them—are going out two by two to help the Kingdom of God come near in the homes where they go. Part of the purpose is to discuss finances on these visits, to give those who are able to give generously an opportunity to do so, and those who are not able to do so to do what they can in good conscience do so that the work of the church—

St. James' Church, the diocese, the national church—may go forward with strength.

It does not seem quite accurate to describe these canvassers as "lambs who are being sent out in the midst of wolves." Some of the canvassers, as a matter of fact, are not very lamb-like. And while there are undoubtedly some wolfish instincts among some of the parishioners, it is obviously untrue to label them wolves. There is, however, for all of us—canvassers, clergy, laity, parishioners—a common experience and a single question: How shall we answer the knock on the door?

When the knock comes or the telephone rings and we ask, "Who is there?" the answer is, "This is Mr. and Mrs. Jones. We are here, or we would like to come, to talk about our common life as ordinary Christian people in the corporate life of this congregation."

The phrase Jesus used was, "The Kingdom of God is near at hand." When Mr. and Mrs. Jones do come and the door is opened and they do speak about belonging to the life of this congregation, the Kingdom of God is near at hand.

When they talk about people in this church accepting one another because they belong to one another—the Kingdom of God is already near. It is there.

When they talk about healing people who are hurt; when they talk about the poor, the deprived, those living distorted lives through no fault of their own; and when they point to the responsibility of those who are not poor, not deprived, not distorted, to help the healing process—they are in fact bringing the Kingdom of God into that apartment.

When they listen to those they call on, hear their concerns, sense their hurts, and share as they are able their burdens—the Kingdom of God is there. When they talk about the worship of the church, how it might be made more holy because they are searching for some sense of holiness and meaning in their lives—the Kingdom of Heaven is there. When they talk about the children and parents and how the church might be of help for young people and older people to grow in grace as they grow in age and in the knowledge and love of God so that they might be increasingly one family—they are already in God's Kingdom. They will not use these exact words, but the words they do use will be the bearers of that Kingdom.

Who is knocking? Just some people, just ordinary people like everybody else. They are knocking to bring some sense of God's presence because they know already in some mysterious way that we all belong to one another in God's Kingdom.

Jesus' promise to his canvassers that some would receive his representatives and some would reject them was certainly carried out in that first Every Member Canvass. Some accepted his Kingdom and some did not. It has also been borne out in the experience of every canvasser for two thousand years including our own. Within the course of the first week that the canvass has been going on, one canvasser telephoned and asked, "May I come and talk to you about St. James' Church?" The answer was, "Certainly you can come. Come to dinner and bring a friend." Another canvasser, after he had called and asked if he might come and visit to talk about St. James' Church, heard the reply, "No! Go to hell!" and the click of the telephone receiver.

When the Kingdom draws near, it comes as a threat sometimes just as much as a promise. When Jesus says, "I am with you always," this promise sometimes threatens us, and we lock the door. The gospel is not simply an invitation to a new more glorious, happy, genuine life. It is that, but it is so in part because it also comes as a judgment upon us and upon our present life, upon our present scale of values, what we think is worth a good deal of money, where we spend our money, where we waste it.

It should be no surprise that the responses to the knock on the door will be varied as life is varied. Our hidden secret life does not look very pretty sometimes in the light of the new day of the gospel. Yet it is that new day that encompasses the dark night. So we really cannot blame people who say, "Go to hell" and hang up because there is something in us that wants to do the same thing—wants to be let alone.

But there is also something in us that prompts us to invite people to dinner. We know down deep inside of us that we are who we are in part because of who the people around us have been, and that we are able to stand with strength largely because of those who are still with us, who have accepted us, who belong to us, who have forgiven us, those who, once we have judged ourselves or permitted ourselves to be judged, embrace us. That is living. So we like to have a gathering around the dinner table. We belong to one another. At its best the church issues an invitation to its members of a family to sit down together at the heavenly banquet.

It is a great mystery why some people say "Come to dinner," and others say "Go to hell." It is hard to figure out. It is an even greater mystery to try to figure out why we do the same thing. Sometimes it is one or the other, and sometimes it is both together.

Usually what we want for other people is what we get. Usually where we want other people to go is where we end up going—either to dinner or to hell. We go either to dinner in a company of people in touch with one another, or we go into isolation. Isolation is hell. Where we send people is usually where we end up going. That is a great mystery.

So when you ask, "Who is there?" and the answer comes, "It's just Mr. and Mrs. Jones," and you realize there is another voice speaking through their voice that has to do with your eternal destiny, how do you reply—"come to dinner" or "go to hell"?

It is not the money, it is the Kingdom that counts. It is not the finances, it is people. It is not things material, it is the spirit that dwells within things material, the finances and budgets. The Kingdom—the sense of God's presence as we go about our life—is near at hand. It is always amongst us whether we accept it or reject it. It is here. God is here. That Kingdom is borne to us by those Mr. and Mrs. Joneses—two by two—who call and knock on the door.

Do not be surprised, if you open the door and listen—really listen—to find yourself moving into that kingdom. Do not be surprised, if you open the door and listen, to find a deeper self in your listening and then speaking, saying something perhaps that you never believed you would be able to say but which wells up from the depths of your being as you hear the bearers of the Kingdom.

Do not be surprised, if when you do listen, you hear yourself talking from the depths of your being. Do not be surprised, when Mr. and Mrs. Jones get up to leave, to hear yourself saying, "Thanks for coming. Next time come back for dinner."

Do not be surprised, when you open the door in this spirit, to discover that it is you who comes through the door—the self that you know you are. And that as you listen you hear Jesus speaking to you—directly to you.

Do not be surprised, if after Mr. and Mrs. Jones leave, he remains to live in your heart by faith forever after.

Do not be surprised to find yourself next year knocking on somebody else's door. Then, when the voice asks, "Who is there?" you can say, "This is Mr. and Mrs. John Smith calling." But to yourself you can say, "It is Jesus knocking." That is what we are about in this canvass—bringing his Kingdom near, his presence near.

Let us pray.

You stand, Jesus, at the door of our heart and knock. We open the door. We invite you in. As we do so, we thank you not only for the knocking but the opening. Amen.

The Blessing Of
#867 Madison Avenue

—⁓—

The First Sunday after Epiphany,
January 7, 1973

On this day when Bishop Donegan blesses the building adjacent to St. James' Church as a center from which the church's concern and care for the community can be expressed, there are two comments that must first be made.

It is most appropriate, first of all, that Bishop Donegan should be the celebrant in this service of Holy Communion and the one who blesses, in the name of God, this building. It is he who was rector when the parish house was built and dedicated. He comes to us today not only as a longtime friend and again as a member of the clergy staff but also as a representative of the continuity of the church through the ages, symbolized in the historic episcopate. We welcome him again and rejoice in his presence and continued ministry. No matter how effective he once was as rector of this church, and no matter how effective he once was as bishop of this diocese, he is certainly now the most effective bishop "retired" in Christendom.

Secondly, it is most appropriate that the Epistle, Gospel, and Intercessions today should be read by the junior and senior wardens and by the vestry chairman of the community committee of this church. They represent the lay leadership of this congregation. They have been responsible, both personally and as officers of the church, for the purchase of this building and for the beginning of the program that will take place there. In particular, if it had not been for Mr. Michel, the senior warden—his immediate response to the opportunity to buy the building, his vision to see how it might be used to the benefit of both the church and the community, and his perseverance in assuring its initial financial base—we would not be having this dedication today, or probably ever. He and those lay men and lay women of this church associated with him on the vestry and in the committees of the church have made this day possible. They represent the Christian church in the contemporary world at its best.

The text that is associated with this event today is a very simple and direct one. It has to do with a city and with a congregation of people in that city who believe in God. The city is Babylon. The people are the Jews. The setting of the text is a few years after 598 B.C. when Jerusalem had been sacked by Nebuchadnezzar, and the Jews taken captive, brought to Babylon, and placed in what we would call "protective custody." The text is taken from a letter written by one of those who stayed in Jerusalem in the rubble—the prophet Jeremiah. He wrote to those exiles in that strange city, and this is what he says: "The Lord says: 'Seek the welfare of the city where I have sent you into exile, and pray to the Lord on its behalf, for in its welfare you will find your welfare'" (Jeremiah 29:7).

The words are without any ambiguity whatsoever. "This city," God says, "is where you have been sent. I have sent you there. No matter what you may think of the city, no matter what you may think of the strange foreigners in that city, or the way in which you were transported to that city, I am the one responsible for your being there."

The members of St. James' Church have been sent to this city and to this corner of it. You are here because God sent you. Out of the intricate mystery of your personal lives, through the mixed motivations that have carried you to come to worship in this place with these people, you have been called by God, drawn by his Spirit. He has by faith sent you here. And no matter what you may think of the city—either its grandeur or its brutality—and no matter what you may consider the reason for your being here—because you love it or because you have to earn a living—the one who has brought you here is God.

Jeremiah and Jesus say the same word: Where you are now is where God wants you to be. Perhaps not forever—but now; he has brought you here.

The reason you are here in this city is to seek its welfare. As people of God, you believe in God. You are identified with the city in which you live. Christians are always identified with the people who surround them.

The great temptation for people who believe they have found God is to huddle together and simply support one another in their own particular religious faith and to look upon those who stand outside their faith as objects for conversion.

It is a very natural temptation and was so for those Jews twenty-six hundred years ago. Jeremiah encouraged his fellow believers to stay together in the practice of their religious faith. Jews are properly very self-conscious of their particular relationship to God, and they are properly offended when they are regarded by members of the Christian faith as objects for conversion. Jeremiah called on them to express their faith, not by converting others, but by seeking the welfare of the city and the people in it.

If we in St James' Church do not seek the welfare of the city—of those in this community in need—we have no right, no right under God, to be here. That is why we are here. We know it. The people of this congregation know it, else we would not have had the unanimous support (apparently) of everyone who belongs to this church in the purchase of this building.

So we start in a very modest way with a ministry to people, most of whom do not belong to this church and never will in all likelihood, and none of whom will we approach with the purpose of making members of this church: elderly people who live alone in cold-water flats; young children whose skins are darker than those of most of this congregation, who have the same ability to learn as our children do; and people who are "troubled" and need counseling help to think through life's decisions and decide which way their lives should go. To begin by helping the well-being of such people as these in a very small way is to seek the welfare of the city.

The church is not and never will be a social welfare agency. We are a congregation of very human people—no better and no worse (generally speaking) than any cross section of people anywhere. But we do know by faith who we are: children of God, members of Christ and (with all mankind) inheritors of his kingdom eternally. The mark of distinction is seen in the sign of the cross at baptism and expressed, not only as we seek the welfare of the city by our actions in it, but as we pray for it. Jeremiah said to those exiles in that enemy town, "Pray for it; pray for those oppressors; pray for those foreigners; pray for those whose culture is different, whose language is different, whose manners are different. You are there to seek their welfare and to pray for them."

What, after all, is the distinctive activity that goes on in this building of the people of St. James' Church in this block between Seventy-First Street and Seventy-Second Street between Madison Avenue and Park Avenue? What do we do that other people do not do when they gather together? The only thing we do together distinctively is pray. What we are here to do above all these other things, but including them all, is to pray to God that we, with other citizens of goodwill, may assure the city's welfare.

So on this first Sunday after Epiphany when we are reminded that Christ goes out as the light of the world to serve the world and to bring life and hope and healing and warmth to the lives of people of the nations, of all cities and all men, we celebrate our prayer and sacrifice of thanksgiving in this service of Holy Communion. Our welfare is here in him who so loved the world that he gave himself. So in a very modest way we pray that we may give ourselves to the welfare of the city and, in its welfare, find our own.

In all that we do in our work and in our prayer may it be to the glory of him who over the generations has brought St. James' Church to where it is and us to where we are in this generation, in this city, in this corner of it. May it become increasingly a corner of God's kingdom. Amen.

Theologian in the White House: The Religion of Abraham Lincoln

—⁂—

The Sixth Sunday after Epiphany, February 11, 1973

A braham Lincoln: Theologian in the White House. That is the theme of this sermon or perhaps more accurately, the theme of this address, for he will very largely speak for himself. It is based on his interpretation of American history symbolized in the phrase that he used at Gettysburg, "This nation under God."

First of all, two aspects of his religion should be identified: one, his negative attitude toward church membership and denominational doctrines; and secondly, his affirmative attitude toward the Bible. "That I am not a member of any Christian church is true," he wrote in 1846, "but I have never denied the truth of the Scriptures; and I have never spoken with intentional disrespect of religion in general, or of any denomination in particular."

Some years later he commented about the matter of creedal affirmations, "When any church will inscribe over its altar as its sole qualification of membership the Savior's condensed statement of the substance of both the law and gospel—Thou shalt love the Lord thy God with all thy heart, and with all thy soul, and with all thy mind, and thy neighbor as thyself—that church will I join with all my heart and soul."

As for the Bible, which according to tradition was the only book in his home when he was a boy, the book which clearly nurtured his personal faith and enabled him to come to his interpretation of God's relationship to this nation, he wrote, "In regard to this Great Book, I have but to say, it is the best gift God has given to man. All the good the Savior gave to the world was communicated through this book. But for it we could not know right from wrong. All things most desirable for man's welfare, here and hereafter, are to be found portrayed in it."

He later said, ". . . the Bible is the only one that claims to be God's Book—to comprise his law, his history. . . . It describes a Governor omnipotent enough to operate this great machine, and declares that he made it . . . I decided a long time ago that it was less difficult to believe that the Bible was what it claimed to be than to disbelieve it. It is a good book for us to obey . . ."

To an old skeptical friend who said that he could not accept the truths of the Bible, he responded in this scene described by the friend himself, Joshua Speed: "Looking me earnestly in the face, and placing his hand on my shoulder, he said, 'You are wrong, Speed; take all of the Book upon reason that you can, and the balance on faith, and you will live and die a happier and better man.'"

Grounded in the Bible without membership in any church (though very regular in week by week attendance at church services, and clearly deeply influenced by a number of clergymen in his lifetime, particularly the Presbyterian minister, the Reverend James Smith in Springfield, who ministered to him when his four-year-old son Edward died) his personal faith grew—that is, his sense of dependence upon God grew and slowly matured.

Listen to these words as he says good-bye to his friends in Springfield on his way to become inaugurated. It is a cold drizzly day in February. He is speaking from the platform of the train:

> My friends—No one, not in my situation, can appreciate my feeling of sadness at this parting. To this place, and the kindness of these people, I owe everything. Here I have lived a quarter of a century, and have passed from a young to an old man. Here my children have been born, and one is buried. I now leave, not knowing when, or whether ever, I may return, with a task before me greater than that which rested upon Washington. Without the assistance of that Divine Being who ever attended him, I cannot succeed. With that assistance, I cannot fail. Trusting in him who can go with me, and remain with you, and be everywhere for good, let us confidently hope that all will yet be well. To his

care commending you, as I hope in your prayers you will commend me, I bid you an affectionate farewell.

It was out of that personal faith, nurtured in part by the crises of his own life—the death of his son and the death of his friends—but then nurtured even more deeply as he began to face crisis after crisis together with the people of the country, as he was drawn deeper and deeper into the understanding of what God was doing in this nation, that his faith as a Christian grew. He was forced to wrestle with the question of what God's Providence meant for the American people. Was God judging the nation because of the wrongs of slavery? Was he going to forgive those who attempted to become reconciled to one another? What was the Gospel of Redemption for a country that was divided? How could God be working his purpose out?

In this wrestling he came in time to have some understanding of God's plan and to see himself, as he said, "an humble instrument in the hands of the Almighty." He once commented to a friend, "I have been driven many times upon my knees by the overwhelming conviction that I had nowhere else to go."

It was out of this agony of prayer that the Emancipation Proclamation was created and decided upon. At the cabinet meeting on September 22, 1862, as the meeting drew to a close, he commented to those gathered there, "I made a solemn vow before God, that if General Lee was driven back from Pennsylvania, I would crown the result by the declaration of freedom to the slaves."

Here is his description of this after the Battle of Gettysburg when he is visiting a hospital in Washington. General Sickles, who lost his leg in that battle, asked Lincoln if he were afraid. Lincoln replied this way:

No, I was not; some of my cabinet and many others in Washington were, but I had no fears . . . I will tell you how it was. In the pinch of the campaign up there, when everybody seemed panic-stricken, and nobody could tell what was going to happen, oppressed by the gravity of our affairs, I went to my room one day, and I locked the door, and got down on my knees before Almighty God, and prayed to him mightily for victory at Gettysburg. I told him that this was his war, and our cause, his cause, but we couldn't stand another Fredericksburg or Chancellorsville. And I then and there made a solemn vow to Almighty God, that if he would stand by our boys at Gettysburg, I would stand by him. And he did stand by your boys, and I will stand by him. After that

(I don't know how it was, and I can't explain it), soon a sweet comfort crept into my soul that God Almighty had taken the whole business into his own hands and that things would go all right at Gettysburg. And that is why I had no fears.

Once that vow and covenant had been made by him and God, and the decision reached, the proclamation delivered and carried out, it is almost as though his religious understanding and conviction immediately matured and deepened. He became committed to the proposition that God was involved, that he was just as involved as the people of the country were involved. In this terrible struggle, God was agonizing as much as the nation was agonizing. He was judging the evil of slavery that his cause of freedom and justice would triumph. God would triumph, and it behooved the people of the nation to be on his side, not to persuade him to their side; but that those who did stand on his side would triumph so that a finer nation might rise.

"I know," he once said to a clergyman in a delegation visiting him, "that the Lord is always on the side of the right. But it is my constant anxiety and prayer that I and the nation should be on the Lord's side."

He said it at Gettysburg:

> It is for the living, rather, to be here dedicated to the great task remaining before us—that from these honored dead we take increased devotion to that cause for which they gave the last full measure of devotion—that we here highly resolve that these dead shall not have died in vain—that this nation, under God, shall have a new birth of freedom—and that government of the people, by the people, for the people, shall not perish from the earth.

The culmination of this faith, of this prophetic vision, his understanding of what it meant to belong to what he called "the Almost Chosen People of God," was set forth finally in that Second Inaugural Address:

> Both parties deprecated war; but one of them would make war rather than let the nation survive; and the other would accept war rather than let it perish. And the war came . . . Neither anticipated that the cause of the conflict might cease with, or even before, the conflict itself should cease. Each looked for an easier triumph, and a result less fundamental and astounding. Both read the same Bible, and pray to the same God; and each invokes his aid against the other. It may seem strange that any

men should dare to ask a just God's assistance in wringing their bread from the sweat of other men's faces; but let us judge not that we be not judged. The prayers of both could not be answered; that of neither has been answered fully. The Almighty has his own purposes. "Woe unto the world because of offenses! For it must needs be that offenses come; but woe to that man by whom the offense cometh!" If we shall suppose that American Slavery is one of those offenses which, in the providence of God, must needs come, but which, having continued through his appointed time, he now wills to remove, and that he gives to both North and South, this terrible war, as the woe due to those by whom the offense came, shall we discern therein any departure from those divine attributes which the believers in a Living God always ascribe to Him? Fondly do we hope—fervently do we pray—that this mighty scourge of war may speedily pass away. Yet, if God wills that it continue, until all the wealth piled by the bonds-man's two hundred and fifty years of unrequited toil shall be sunk, and until every drop of blood drawn with the lash, shall be paid with another drawn with the sword, as was said three thousand years ago, so still must be said "the judgments of the Lord, are true and righteous altogether."

With malice toward none; with charity for all; with firmness in the right, as God gives us to see the right, let us strive on to finish the work we are in; to bind up the nation's wounds; to care for him who shall have borne the battle, and for his widow, and his orphan to do all which may achieve and cherish a just and lasting peace, among ourselves, and with all nations.

How did he regard that message himself? In a letter to Thurlow Reed he gave this interpretation: "I expect [it] to wear as well as—perhaps better than—anything I have produced; but I believe it is not immediately popular. Men are not flattered by being shown that there has been a difference of purpose between the Almighty and them. To deny it, however, in this case, is to deny that there is a God governing the world. It is a truth which I thought needed to be told; and as whatever of humiliation there is in it, falls most directly on myself, I thought others might afford for me to tell it."

A great Christian statesman. More than that in that letter—a great Christian soul in the White House. There is a God governing the world. There is a God governing the nation. We can give thanks to God for sending him as an instrument of his purpose. We may pray that we may in our day be instruments for the same purpose.

Theologian in the White House. Christian in the White House. Saint now, as he believed, in Heaven. May his spirit and the spirit which possessed him possess those now in the White House and in the positions of government in our land, and in our city, and in ourselves. Amen.

The Story of Jesus Christ: His Birth

—m—

The First Sunday in Lent,
March 11, 1973

Christ was born in the year 4 BC and died in the year 28 AD—give or take one or two years. He was brought up in a middle class, artisan family in Nazareth, a small town in a province of the Roman Empire, Galilee.

The only recorded incident of the growing-up years was a pilgrimage that he took with his parents on one of the high holy days of the Jewish faith to pray in the Temple in Jerusalem.

At about the age of thirty he began to go around the countryside from town to town talking about the coming Kingdom of God, explaining what he thought its nature to be, teaching the reality of God expressed in that Kingdom, and its effect upon men and women who are living their lives on earth. He drew about him in a particularly close relationship twelve men who became his disciples and to whom he revealed his innermost thoughts.

He did this for approximately three years. As he described the reality of God as he knew it, he increasingly earned the enmity of the religious leaders, who considered his teaching blasphemy, and the suspicion of the political leaders. Finally the enmity and the suspicion became so great that he was put to death in Jerusalem, accused of both blasphemy and treason. This death Jesus had already anticipated and had tried to prepare his disciples for by saying that after he had been put to death he would be raised from the dead and that they were, therefore, to trust him.

In the days following his death, first the disciples and then gradually an increasing number of people—in excess finally of five hundred—became convinced that he had in fact been raised from the dead, that he had spoken the truth, that he was alive. They experienced his presence. What he had said would come to pass, had come to pass. It was after the resurrection that they came to trust him. They gradually began to see that there was nothing they ever had to fear anymore—not even their deaths. Nobody, when they really trusted him, could do anything to them that would destroy them.

As they tried to describe to those who had not known Jesus exactly the quality of this experience, the words that they came to use most frequently were, "Jesus is Lord." He is in charge. The reality of the universe is expressed in him. God and his Kingdom is the reality with which we have to reckon the rest of our lives. The way to reckon with that reality is to trust him. They said, "Trust him; you will find him trustworthy. In that trust you will find your life."

In varying degrees that has been the experience of Christians for two thousand years, including the experience of many of you who are here this morning—imperfectly, with ambiguities, but it is a reality you know.

We begin, therefore, this Lent a series of sermons on Jesus Christ—his story from his birth to his resurrection—in order that the knowledge of him that you already have may be deepened; and if you do not have much knowledge, or even any knowledge, that it may at least be begun. The purpose of the sermons: that you might *know* him; so that the experience of the first century Christians may become in some measure our experience in the twentieth century.

To come to this knowledge we shall use two sources throughout the series: one source is the story told by his disciples and those who directly followed them for approximately that one hundred years after the resurrection. We will try to get inside the knowledge that they had of Jesus Christ as they explained it. That explanation is in the New Testament. That is one source: the story they tell. We shall listen to them.

The other source is *ourselves*. Knowledge of Jesus Christ is always a personal knowledge. It is a knowledge that arises out of his presence now among us and within us as we trust him. It is in that respect exactly the same today as it was then—no difference whatsoever. So we shall listen not only to the disciples, but we shall listen to ourselves to hear the same story (as the hymn has it) "of Jesus and his love." We will learn from our life together and our own inner lives.

We begin this morning with his birth. As we begin, as all stories should, at the beginning, we discover that his birth is *not* the beginning. The beginning, say the authors of the New Testament, was not when Jesus was born in Bethlehem, but rather when the world was born. That is where Christ has been since before the beginning. The disciples said, "When we saw him as a man we saw in him the power that had been from the beginning of all creation." He is the power behind the process of evolution when it started and has been involved in that process ever since. That is the one we lived with.

He was born just at the right time so he could be himself. He was born, they said, "in the fullness of time" to reveal the character of the universe, of God. Before his birth a period of preparation went on for billions of years. Mankind had to be prepared by millions of years of evolving out of nothing finally into *homo sapiens*—a created being who had a mind and could think, who came to recognize the difference between right and wrong and decide for one or the other, who emerged finally from his tribal life in the caves, from a nomadic life, to a pastoral agricultural life, to an urban life. All the laws developed by the societies of men to hold people together in some kind of a rough justice, and all the visions men had of what justice might become and how people might live together in harmony, all those visions expressed by poets and prophets—these were summed up in the One who was the law and the prophets, a member of the Jewish people who had a special gift of wrestling with eternal meaning and the mystery of human existence. It was as a member of that race that he came to be born at a particular time which was "the fullness of time."

He came to a particular people for all mankind. He came as Man (with a capital "M"). He had two characteristics as Man: reality and compassion, truth and love. He came as the foundation of the world expressed in love. He came as God and man. All together: the particular and the universal, the earthly and the eternal, the human and the divine.

This is the story the disciples are trying to tell—the story of how the immortal, invisible, all-powerful God came to earth to live a mortal, visible, powerless life as a baby. In Jesus they met the reality of God so that they could say, "The truth of existence is that compassion is more powerful than anything else—more powerful than even your sin or your death. Trust that compassionate, graceful love which you experience in your own lives. Trust it. Live it. That is to participate in eternal life because that is the way eternity is. You already have it. It is right here. You don't have to do anything to earn it or to get it. It is given. What you have was most uniquely given in Jesus Christ."

So when they presented the story of Jesus, they did not refer so much to what his teachings were or what he did; they presented *him*. They did not so much urge their hearers to imitate him and to become good people as to trust him and who he was. His message, in other words, was *himself*.

The question then: What did he think of himself? How did he consider that self? Who did he think he was?

The uniqueness of Jesus consisted in the consciousness of an utterly unique relationship with God. The relationship was that of a son to a father. No one knows the father, he says, except his son. No one knows the son except the father. The knowledge of God that I have is the unique knowledge that a son has of a father, and I am going to give that knowledge to those who trust me. If you trust me, you will know.

To give that love was his mission; to bring God's reality to life by participating in God's will, obedient to the motions of compassion and love day by day, moment by moment. In his total life, death, and resurrection, he emerged *the* Man in whom the reality of all creation dwells. He knew who he was, that he had a special purpose, so he lived his life through everything that came, including his death, uniquely *himself*.

He did so for one purpose only—that you and I might lead our lives uniquely *ourselves*. One way to come to this knowledge of him is to listen to his story told by his disciples, reflect upon it, regard it. The other way is to listen to yourself. Read the story of your life. Regard it with attention. Something is going on to heed and to attend. The quality of what is going on in your life is the quality that was expressed most fully in his life.

How can you do this? You can do it as you sense within yourself the movement of that spirit which is uniquely yours and move in relationship to that spirit which is yours and yours absolutely alone—Mary Jones and John Smith—nobody else ever like you, ever. Your life is in relationship to that spirit. The only way that you can live is to live in accordance with that spirit, not in accordance with somebody else's. That destroys you. You were born just at the right time—"the fullness of time"—just at the right time, the only time for you to be the person you are known to be—to be an individual responsible to yourself and to God.

You were born just the way Jesus Christ was born: out of the love of God from before the foundation of the world—and in the very particular, personal circumstances of your mother and of your father, the heritage that is yours, the village where you were born, or the city, in that particular setting you share the universal life of God.

As you are touched with that spirit and obey that spirit, you will be wholly yourself. Anything else is to prostitute yourself, to adulterate yourself, to make yourself less than you are. You are responsible only to that spirit. That is God's spirit. That is to be responsible unto God.

So the final question is: Can you then live now so that you are conscious of being a unique individual and, therefore, conscious of your eternal responsibility before God?

Of course you can. That is why you are here. You can become yourself more wholly right now. Or if you have never been yourself, you can begin to become yourself. You can live more consciously yourself as you are more conscious day by day of your relationship to God. That is to have personal knowledge of Christ. If you have never thought of yourself in this way, or if you have never read your own story this way, this is the day you can begin to take on a new self-understanding and therefore a new life because you have begun to have this kind of relationship to him, this kind of a knowledge of him.

This is why Christ was born—that you might be reborn in him, to take on deeper and deeper individuality with your own unique integrity. He lived, died, and rose again uniquely himself so that you might live, die, and rise again eternally uniquely yourself now. That is when eternal life begins. Now.

Trust him. Be yourself, and trust him. Don't settle for anything else. That is to *know* him. That is to *live* him. That is in fact to *be* him. Then you are wholly yourself.

Let us pray:

Lord Jesus, when we know you a little bit, we trust you a little bit. We thank you for the little knowledge you have given us. We hope we may trust you more and more. Help us to know you day by day as we trust you so that you may give us more and more of yourself. Let us not worry overmuch about who is for us or agrees with us, or who is against us and disagrees. Let us not worry too much about who understands us, or who turns his back. Rather may we see to it that in everything we do, we do it with you and in your spirit. Amen.

The Story of Jesus Christ:
His Trial (Mark 15:1–20)

—m—

Good Friday, April 20, 1973

That night Jesus spent in a cell in the home of the high priest. In the morning, after further consultation, the priests, scribes, and elders decided to turn Jesus over to Pontius Pilate, the Roman governor, with the charge that he claimed to be the King of the Jews and that since they had no king but Caesar, Jesus should therefore be charged with the death penalty.

It is interesting (and all too depressing a business because it is all too common) to note the easy abdication of religious responsibility to political authority. The Jewish leaders in fact had the authority to stone Jesus to death because of his blasphemy. Rather than make that decision and live with it, whatever the consequences, as mature people are meant to do (to make mature decisions and live with them), they backed away and said, "We'll let Pilate do it. We'll pressure him to have him put Jesus to death on political grounds. Then we will not be guilty, but he will be."

The word "religion" comes from the Latin word *religio,* to bind together. The business of religion is the business of binding people together with one another and with God. Whatever that religion is, its concern is the relationship that binds God and men together. The Christian religion maintains that the fullest expression of that relationship is in Christ. He maintained in his teaching and in his ministry and in himself that God's kingdom is meant to rule the hearts and the minds of men. That rule is expressed as men and women are bound together in love and as every society is built upon justice. It is as clear and as simple as that. Therefore, anything that expresses love and justice–anything, not just religious things but any aspect of life where there is love and where justice prevails—is an expression of a religious motivation and concern. Therefore, naturally, anything that stands *against* love and justice and prevents or violates them is a matter of religious concern.

For religious forces to abdicate their responsibility to try to determine and therefore express what God's will is for his people is a renunciation of what it is to be God's representatives and to claim to speak in the name of religion. I say "try to determine" because any religious interpretation is given by very fallible men and women and their political judgment may be wrong. To be a man of religion does not necessarily bring any political insights into what is true. Indeed, one of the perspectives of religion is to be able to see that nonreligious men sometimes are better representatives politically of God's rule than religious men.

Their basic religious concern is always, however, very simple and very all-inclusive—that everything that affects man affects God. Therefore, God is concerned about every aspect of man's life from the cradle to the grave, and before the cradle, the womb. That is as much God's womb as it is the woman's womb, or the man's who put the seed in the womb. For religious men to say that is a matter of the state is an abdication of their responsibility. What they determine to be the right life or how they judge the termination of life in the womb may be subject to wide disagreement and diversity, but the fact that God is there is the affirmation that God is the God of life—and, of course, death. God is God. He is to be involved in the lives of men. He is to be obeyed in every area of life where his kingdom is meant to reign. Where his kingdom reigns is wherever man lives—the kinds of houses he lives in, the kinds of houses he can't get into, the kinds of houses that decay, the kinds of houses that have rats, the kinds of schools his children go to, the kind of family life that his children belong to, and the kind of political life he lives, because all men are political animals. These are all God's. Those fundamental human issues of how men and women live together in society are finally always moral issues, and as such they are God's business and therefore the business of religion as well as of politics.

Perhaps when the Gibbons of the future writes "The Decline and Fall of America," he will point out that one of the reasons for that fall was the decline in the sense of moral outrage against injustice, against corruption, against the big lie, against manipulation of opinion as of stocks; and that one of the reasons for that was the abdication of the religious forces of America of their responsibility to witness to "One nation under

God" and to hand all decisions affecting man's life in the nation over to the state and the political leaders and to say that religion is concerned only about man's personal morality.

Religion is not simply a private matter of one's personal relationship to God—although it is that. It is a corporate matter of how men living together reflect the characteristics of the kingdom of God in some measure creating a society which makes it possible for love to be expressed and compassion to go on and undergird human affairs, for justice to be in the law courts as well as safety in the streets, for equality of opportunity, and dedication to serve the state, not to manipulate it or to ask to be served by it. That is treason! A church which abdicates is a cowardly church. A cowardly church crucifies Christ day after day. A Church more concerned about itself than its mission, more concerned about its inner life than the life of God in the world is a crucifying church.

Who, then, to return to the trial, was responsible for the death of Jesus? Certainly not the Jewish people. So far as we can determine, the Jewish people—that is, the rank and file of them, the common people— in the words of one reporter, "heard Jesus gladly." They flocked around him. He was followed everywhere by crowds of ordinary citizens who, while certainly not understanding who he was, knew he was someone who healed sick people, who fed hungry people, who loved little children, who called peace-makers the "blessed ones," and said that he would lay down his life for everybody. Furthermore, Jesus said if you lay down your life for people and live in that spirit, then you have got to be able to live in a way that you never could live before. That struck a chord in the hearts of these very ordinary people. Why wouldn't the Jewish people respond by being glad to be in his company? No, it wasn't the Jews who were responsible for his death.

Nor was it Pilate. We like to think that if we could put our finger on the head of the state and say, "He is the guilty one," no matter what the wrong doing, then we could be certain that justice would be done. Never true. Pilate was not responsible. Pilate happened to be the one in office who ordered the crucifixion, but he never would have done it if the prisoner had not been delivered to him by the abdication of the religious authorities. Pilate was an administrator. His job was to keep the peace. Though humanly speaking it seems in those gospel accounts that he may have wanted to save Jesus because he saw that it was for envy that the priests had delivered him, he was more concerned, as administrators usually are, to save himself and the power of his office. So he gave way finally to the pressures of the crowd that had been stirred up by the religious authorities. In order to keep the peace, he ordered Jesus' death. How ironical that it was this death and resurrection which, in a few short years, turned, as the gospel says, "the world upside down"—Pilate's world, the world of the Romans. Pilate was weak, but neither in himself nor in his office was he responsible for the death of Jesus. It is never political office or the holders of political office who are responsible for evil, though they may give way to certain pressures. Who then is?

It is hard to avoid the conclusion that there is something in the human race—in all of us—which is really set against love and does not like it, and will kill it if it can. We see in ourselves the same envy the priests had for position and power and prestige. They wanted to control life. We want to control life. They wanted to speak in the name of God and nobody else, and that is what we want to do. If we have something, we do not want to give it away. We certainly do not want to have it taken away. We have the same tendency to dodge responsibility that Pilate had. We do not want to be involved. We like to wash our hands of any responsibility if someone is going to get hurt and we might be blamed for it. We all know what it is like to give way to pressures the way Pilate did, to fail to speak the truth when we know it. We tend to identify with the pack that we travel with. We tend, in fact, to become like other members of the pack, and therefore moral chameleons—to be one person with one pack, and another person with another pack, just moving from pack to pack or place to place.

So when we look at that scene at the trial and try to put ourselves in the places of those who were carrying out the drama, we can sympathize with all of them. We resent love in the measure that we are unlovable. We resist justice in the measure to which we are unjust. When the loving God comes into our life with his justice, he is unbearable; when he comes as love—pure, unadulterated, self-sacrificing love—we abhor him, and we want to kill him.

But God will not stay killed. He keeps coming back. The resurrection happens day after day. No matter what we do, or how much we hate, or how we kill, or destroy, or back away from responsibilities, or how we point our fingers at everybody else, God's love—God's unbearable love—is finally unbeatable. No matter how we respond, or what we do, or who we are, he keeps coming back gladly, persistently, gracefully, saying, "You are loved. I love you. The reality of eternity is that you are loved and will always be loved no matter what you do. I am going to keep on coming until you learn to love me."

So we can't cast stones and say, "You over there are responsible for killing Jesus." That is something that we all are responsible for because there is something in us that wants that. We confess it.

To whom then shall we turn? Look at that scene: the riled-up crowds, the frantic priests, the wavering Pilate. The only person not riled-up, not frantic, not weak is Jesus, in complete possession of himself in the middle of the tumult. He doesn't even have to defend himself, or apologize for himself, or explain himself. His defense is who he is. His defense is simply his interior life, doing the will of God as he knows it. He is secure—secure in that inner integrity where he is obedient to love—the only one who not only would never kill love, but obey it right down to his death. He had once commanded it as the rule of life and of all men in every society and now he was to obey it. He had committed himself to accomplish the work that he had been sent to do. He is in God.

In our frantic, riled-up, weak, wavering, fuzzy lives, to whom can we turn? He is the only one. He is the only one who has that inner resource that we know we need and in fact, when we obey it, know we possess it. In him forgiven, given peace; in him born to new life, borne always to the Cross, never avoiding it.

In a sense if we can really turn from our inner lives and move into his inner life and with him see what it means to open ourselves to God, pressing upon him, to be obedient to love and to strive for justice and to want above all else to do just that, then we are led into the heart of the greatest mystery of all—the heart of the mystery of God himself.

Finally, the one ultimately responsible for the Crucifixion is God. That is the mystery. In the Cross he expressed what was in his mind from before the beginning of the world—his unifying love for his creation, for all men, for you and for me to be at one with him. He will in fact in his son die to express it so that love can rise in our hearts eternally.

On Returning from Vacation

—⁓—

The Fourteenth Sunday after Trinity,
September 23, 1973

Our good friend and neighbor, Dr. [David H.C.] Read of the Madison Avenue Presbyterian Church, has pointed out that when a clergyman goes on vacation, he becomes just like a layman so far as his religion is concerned. That is, he no longer is forced professionally to think about religious matters. He no longer has to prepare sermons or call on the sick and dying. He no longer has to pray in public. He does not have to be concerned about the structure of the services of worship. He does not even have to write letters to parishioners asking for financial support. He is freed from vocational ties when he is on vacation.

This change—for me, and I imagine for most clergy—comes as a welcome period of refreshment. What is subject to professionalism becomes personal once again. The necessity—a proper necessity—to be professional, or to be as professional as possible, and therefore as responsible as possible, to be at least responsible professionally as a clergyman—as a doctor or teacher or businessman is meant to be professional—that proper necessity is lifted on vacation so that the appropriation of the Christian faith personally may be enriched by tapping deeper sources or new sources for the renewal of one's own personal religious life. As a doctor or a teacher or a businessman or lawyer returns from vacation refreshed to carry on his professional life, so a clergyman. He returns having been renewed in what he professes to believe.

So, in fact, this first sermon is "On Returning from Vacation." It was meant to be preached last Sunday, but as you will remember we had the unexpected pleasure of having Archbishop [Ted] Scott* with us so it has been renewed and reworked for this Sunday. The title seems a little distant now, as though vacation had come to an end a long time ago rather than two weeks ago. It is a little more personal a sermon than most sermons preached from this pulpit but that may be the purpose of a vacation—to get personal renewal and to share those personal reflections.

That renewal came in three ways: first, just simply physical renewal. I could not imagine how poorly I looked last June until I discovered people saying how well I looked in September: a recognition that our body is largely a temporary shelter which ought to be renewed from time to time, to be repaired so the spirit can be repaired. When the body breaks down it is easier for the spirit to break down; when it is in good repair the spirit that it houses is more apt to be in good spirit. So a vacation means physical exercise and physical exhaustion at the end of the day rather than nervous and emotional exhaustion: long hours walking on the beach, swimming, playing tennis—playing tennis as hard as one can, and finally being beaten by one's oldest son. It is a humbling experience, and yet one is also a little proud of him when after you congratulate him he says, "Well, I've been waiting 29 years for this day!" Physical renewal.

Intellectual renewal. Most of my reading this summer was on Eastern religions: Hinduism, Buddhism, and Taoism—in part to try to be intelligent in conversations with that older son whose field this is in graduate school, but more importantly, an attempt to try to go beyond the surface in searching for the renewal of the religious spirit in so many young people in American life today. Out of this came a renewed sense of our participation in nature, of our belonging to a process which goes on all through time and all through existence—the pounding of the surf in the evening and the surf still pounding in the morning; eons ago it was pounding and long after we leave this shore for another shore the pounding will continue. Belonging to that process, through the reality of everything and the void of nothingness—as we participate in that process in our own lives we both transform the reality and are transformed by it. We all are in some measure a part of that passage, that way, from mystery through reality to mystery and the reality that hides behind the void of nothingness. Thus the sense of renewal, of our belonging together—part of the cycle of nature—and of our being carried

*Primate of Canada, 1971–1986

everlastingly along this way. There is so much more to the movement of our life than the passion of our little decisions as to how they will carry us. We are carried by that spirit who is in, and lives through, that process from everlasting to everlasting.

When Jesus said, "I am the Way," he was saying, in effect, "I am the way of birth, and life, and death, and life again, and I touch all who are in the process because I am that process." So the Incarnation.

I know that many Christian people would not agree with this statement but it seems to me that all people who strive in their own religious tradition and religious ways to be in touch with the Eternal Spirit are already, in fact, in touch with Jesus. Therefore our task as Christians is not to convert them but to affirm them in their own understanding of religious truth and the Way. As they are in the Way, we should be free to believe they will come to know him who also said, "I am the Truth." So the Christian religion does not set itself over against other religions but at its best completes them. Our task is to enter as sympathetically as we can into other traditions as well as into the lives of those who belong in part to the Christian faith but are unable to accept what they call its "dogmas" and "absolutism."

The only absolute is the Way. And if you are in the Way, then you will come to the Truth and the Life—that is the Eternal Spirit moving through all of life. So physical renewal, intellectual renewal, finally spiritual renewal.

The whole purpose in recognizing the religious dimension in life is to recognize the life of the spirit: like any spirit, one's attitude toward life, one's style of living, one's way of dying and facing death. The physical body and the mind—important as they are—ultimately turn to ashes and dust, but our spirits living in that body and mind become increasingly a part of the Spirit which is eternal. So the renewal of the spirit.

How can it be brought about? We cannot bring it about, but it can be brought about: God brings it about. We wait upon him and, if we can, participate in his spirit as we discern that spirit. To participate in that spirit is to make decisions in your life in accordance with what you believe is right, as you understand that right under God, and then to live in that spirit, as well as you can, or more accurately, to let that spirit live in you. That spirit is, if we will be alert to it, always pressing upon us because that is its character—to belong to it, to participate in it, to be loyal to it, to listen to it—and when we hear it, to obey it. Obey him—that is life in the Spirit!

There is always a growing edge in everybody's life and to be in touch with that growing edge is where the Spirit is at work. There is always some point of renewal. What it is for me may be one thing; what it is for you may be another thing; and what it is for everybody else under the sun may be something else again. But for everyone there is—if he has eyes to see and ears to hear—a calling of the Spirit to renew one's own spirit, permitting that spirit to determine your decisions, living it as well as you can day by day, so that you are having dealings not simply with people and the exigencies of life but with the Eternal Spirit.

So where is the Spirit touching your spirit? Where is your heart being pressed? Where are you being hounded by something or someone? Where do you believe you can become more yourself than you are? Where are you seeing more clearly what is right in order that you may be more fully yourself and know that you will never be content until you respond, postpone it as you would? What relationship in your life do you know that you have to do something about if you are going to be true to your own spirit and the Eternal Spirit—restore a broken one? forgive? return? embrace? set free?

Where are your fears? What are you most afraid of—being alone? having someone you love desperately sick unto death? wanting to bear the pain of someone else? Let that spirit embrace you and him, or her. Let that spirit temper those fears, accept them, destroy them. Trust that spirit. Then live to the best of your ability and go about your business and let God take the rest.

Where are your hopes? A life that might be lived with a deeper sense of direction, or with a greater conviction, or with a greater meaning? A life that has some underlying sense of peace that is not just a fabric of allegiance? A life that has some sense of confidence—that if you love God things will always work out for good, and the worst you can do is to give up, and the best you can do is to go forward with hope in that Spirit? So you decide in that spirit with that Spirit.

And the God of hope in whom all promises that have ever been held out to you by the Eternal Spirit always answers "yes." And so you sense that while the Spirit is touching you where it is calm, where it is yearning within you, that you may trust him, belong to him, participate in him. Your spirit will be renewed for it is an Eternal Spirit. There is nothing to fear anymore and there is everything to hope for. This is the glory of God—and if you are glorifying God you are helping the people whose lives you touch to live with a stronger renewed spirit themselves.

That, it seems to me, is what the Christian faith is all about. Thanks be to God for vacations!

Let us pray:

Renew, O God, a right spirit within us. Take our fears, and our hopes. Take the people in our lives through whom you will touch us. Then help us to trust you as we obey you—or try to—so may we glorify your Holy Name, world without end. Amen.

Report on the General Convention 1973

—⚏—

The Seventeenth Sunday after Trinity, October 14, 1973

On the evening of the first full day at the General Convention there was a joint session of the two Houses and of the Women's Triennial when the Executive Council was asked to present its program for the next three years. I was asked to conclude that presentation with my understanding of the relationship of the national church to the gospel. This morning—at this time when the gospel is to be preached rather than a report given—I propose to adapt some of those comments to our life here at St. James' Church.

It is perfectly clear that one of the common threads that is woven through all of the life of the church, at the national level, the diocesan level, and the parish level, is the fact that everyone who is involved in the life of the church, in one way or another, has a very fundamental love for the church and concern for its well-being. I am thinking not so much about the love for the One, Holy, Catholic Apostolic Church in the sense of the sweep of history, but rather in terms of loyalty and love for the Episcopal Church in the United States of America and in particular for the churches where we are as parishes—that is, the local "St. James' Church" in every town throughout this country—large or small. This is the church which nourishes and sustains us, which gives us hope and comfort, which annoys us, frustrates us, makes us angry at times; the church which helps us realize that we are forgiven and accepted by God who has given us the sacraments of grace, and which in the turmoil and the anguish, the desperation sometimes of our lives, has lifted our eyes in the direction of heaven and has reminded us that that is where our true home is.

So at the moment, I am speaking about our very ordinary parish life—the women's groups and the men's groups, the prayer groups and the work groups, the spring fairs and the fall canvasses, the search for church school teachers and the church school noises, the joyous celebration that parishes have when a new rector is installed, and sometimes even happier celebration when he leaves. I am pointing to our failures as well as our successes. In our most honest moments, most Episcopalians would confess that their churches make no great impact upon the communities where they are placed and that if their particular church disappeared, the city or town would go on all right. We usually are more concerned about keeping our members, even if they drive thirty miles or more on Sundays, than we are about the kids around the corner who might be in the church building every day. We are parochial in the Episcopal Church, both in the best sense of that word and in the worst.

Yet despite our failures, this weak, sometimes very ineffective, sometimes divided, always limited parish church is where we were made members of Christ in baptism, where we take one another until death parts us in Holy Matrimony, and where we commit into the safe-keeping of God's eternal love those whom we love when they die. It is the parish church that grounds us in the Reality of life and says that Reality is in fact God. So it's a real mish-mash. There is no crystal clear purity. There is quite a lot of darkness and it's all shot through with grace. It is in those personal parish relationships where we have seen bitterness give way to gentleness, sorrows turned into joy, pain transformed into power, where what we learn is what we have suffered.

Out of the depths of our hearts we have sung the glory of God, and sometimes as we have sung, the songs of heaven have echoed and re-echoed in our hearts. We have known at certain moments that no matter what, God is God—and we are safe in him and he wants us to count as people in his world. That is why, I take it, we are here in this church; why people go to their parish churches all over the land; why they support in some measure the diocese and in some measure the national church: our love for the church with all its imperfections.

That our church should leave so much to be desired should not surprise us, for so do we: its imperfections are there because we are imperfect.

We are very temperate in our faith in the Episcopal Church. We do not convert many people. We do not care too much about those people who stand outside us, especially if they are different in color or language or social standing. We have plenty of darkness in our hearts—the very same hearts that love the church. So if we are to think intelligently about the church, we do not begin with the national church (the national *anything* can seldom inspire people); we do not even begin with our local churches—we begin rather with ourselves because the church and we are all of a piece. Division in the national church is no more than a reflection of the division in our own hearts, just as in the same way our love for the church is a reflection of our love for our bishops, dioceses, clergy and parishes, and neighbors and ourselves.

What it comes down to is this: if we are to move ahead with any sense of mission, that is, any sense that there is some significance in the life of the Episcopal Church—*that* will rise from the sense of purpose that each one of us has for his own life. The Church is a Person: Christ. It is made up of persons: you and me. And the wholeness and the direction of his life in the world is bound to the wholeness and the direction of our lives in the world. The power of his mission is determined by the power of our personal lives in our homes and communities and job and churches.

So to ask "What is the Church here for?" is to ask, "What do you think you are here for?" And how you answer the question of your purpose and your meaning will determine the answer to the mission of the church. Therefore, if we are to set things in a right perspective, we will not set up one group over another—those who are concerned about personal religion, for example, over against those who are concerned about social matters. We will not be concerned about simply getting, as they say, the church "back on the track." What is the point of a church getting back on the track if it just sits in the station? Once it's back on the track, where is it going? And where does it get its motive power from? Who gets up the steam? What is its mission?

Sometimes we talk about mission as though it were some esoteric something that we have that we are going to give to those people who do not have it: money or power or education or wealth or housing or our liturgy or the Good News of the gospel. Mission may include any or all of those things, and at different times in the history of the world and the church, there will be different kinds of emphases. But our *essential* mission, and the only one that counts for anything, is our obedience to God—where we are. All else follows from that. The steam for mission rises from personal commitment to Christ and then quiet, persistent obedience to him. This cannot ever be done by conventions—national conventions, diocesan conventions, not even by parish meetings. It begins—you know it and I know it—in the recesses of our hearts. The church becomes whole as we become whole—that is, as we accept and acknowledge and offer the darkness that is within us, the demons that are there, and the delight that we have sometimes in evil.

When the members affirm Christ—worship him, listen to him, are honestly willing to be judged by him, try to obey him and be renewed by him—they will be, the church will be, transformed by him. So, a call to come to a General Convention ends as a call to come home to our parishes and a call to come home to ourselves.

This moving from darkness into light, from division into wholeness, from brokenness into healing, is what Paul was referring to when he said, "He is our Peace." Different, divided sides of our nature are not meant to be denied but meant to be transformed. That transformation is not something that we do; it is something that Christ does. So the renewal of the church rests upon the renewal of St. James' Church, and the renewal of St. James' Church rests upon our renewal. He who is our Peace has made us one. He has made us one that he might create in himself a new person, so making peace.

May that peace be yours, and may that peace belong to the whole church. Then with him in our hearts the next step in the life of the church and in the defining of her mission in our society will be made clear. Who can say what that vision of the church might yet be in bringing healing to our nation, in holding high that love of integrity and honesty and decency and authenticity that men and women might be free men and women in our nation, that the church might capture once again that deep conviction that God is God, that those who obey God will flourish, and that the fullness of life for everyone may be found freely in the understanding that he is the King and that our life is in obedience to him?

So if we can hold the Lord high and lifted up in our own hearts, we can hold him high and lifted up in the life of St. James' Church. That is how he will be held high and lifted up in the life of our nation and of our world.

Let us pray:

Almighty God, we acknowledge the darkness in our hearts and want to expose the depths of those hearts to your light. Let us not be afraid to do this. We acknowledge our separations from those different from us and offer them to you for your healing. We thank you for the knowledge of your love for us in Christ and pray that we may accept him as our Peace and dwell with him as new people—accepting, forgiving, living with him where you have placed us: in this church, in this city, in our families, and in ourselves. Through Christ our Lord. Amen.

St. James' Church and
Its Community

—⁓—

The Eighteenth Sunday after Trinity,
October 21, 1973

The forum that took place at 10 o'clock this morning in the parish
house was called "St. James' Church and its Community." It was a
forum sponsored by the community ministry committee of this parish
and its purpose was to bring to the attention of members of the parish
ways by which they might be involved in helping meet some of the
needs of the people of this community.

Encouragement was given, therefore, as it has been over the years, to
volunteers working through community organizations throughout the
city. There has been, ever since St. James' was founded, generation after
generation of distinguished service provided by thousands of St. James'
people to institutions which provide help to alleviate human suffering—
hospitals, social service and welfare agencies, schools, prisons, day care
centers, recreational programs, family and individual counseling services, and, more recently, housing projects, drug agencies, and institutions that deal with racial injustice. There is available through this
community ministry committee a list of organizations in the city which
welcome volunteer help, and members of the parish are encouraged to
avail themselves of one of these opportunities to serve human need. This
volunteer service that parishioners carry on through ecclesiastical and
secular organizations in the city might be called ordinary Christian cit-
izenship in which Christians take their place alongside members of other
religions—or of no religion—simply to express human compassion, care,
and concern.

In addition to this kind of general participation by the members of the parish, the purchase, renovation, and opening of No. 867 Madison Avenue, our adjacent building, has enabled St. James' Church to participate more directly in the work of several particular agencies which serve the community. Through sharply reduced rental fees, financial support, and in some instances, the active involvement of our parishioners, there is now this additional institutional support from this church for organizations that were created to help the elderly, those who are troubled and need counseling, those who are sick and need to be called on, and those who, because of the city and its structures, need additional help in order to be properly educated.

It is our hope that by June of this year all of the available space in 867 will be occupied by organizations that serve the community and that we shall then have a strong, steady, visible witness in that building that St. James' Church does indeed care for the community of which it is a part and is concerned to strengthen the human condition of all people regardless of their religious convictions, the color of their skin, or their place in our society. They all belong to us and we belong to them because together we all belong to the human community and to God. So in the lives of the members of this parish, in their volunteer services and in their institutional support, may it be perfectly clear that St. James' Church is indeed involved in and cares about the community of which it is a part and is prepared to make sacrifices to express that care.

The question which we now address ourselves to, therefore, is St. James' Church and its community. Where is our community? How do you define it? What are its boundaries? The parishioners of this church come very largely from that area bounded by Fifth Avenue and the East River between Fifty-Fifth and Ninety-Sixth Streets. Is that our community? Or is our community larger than that? Does it extend across the park, and to the north and to the south? Does it take in all of the city, like the Mets do when they are winning? Does it include causes that do not have distinct city or local boundaries, such as International Planned Parenthood, the YM and YWCAs, the Boy Scouts and Girl Scouts? Or can it include the people in the sub-Sahara undergoing what may be the worst famine in the history of the world? Do they belong to our community?

It is a very knotty question, where to draw what lines around which concerns; to determine where we belong as members of what community. You cannot go everywhere, and yet it is clear that you have to go somewhere, to some particular place, to some particular persons or peoples if you are to be honest and effective in your expression of concern for your community. As Christian people we would like our lives to count in the community, to help meet human needs, and to help undergird and strengthen justice and the structures of justice—and yet we cannot keep going so far away that we neglect what is in our own backyard.

The parable of the Good Samaritan may be of help to us. That was Jesus' reply to the question, "Who is my neighbor?" Your neighbor, he said, is the person who is in need. He is the one who is attacked on the Jericho Road, who is mugged, robbed, left for dead, and desperately needs help. If you pass by on the other side, turn your head away, don't want to become involved or inconvenienced, want to avoid all trouble, then you are like those that Jesus condemned—the priests and the Levites—probably very good men who were so busy going about the work of the religious institution that they had no time to meet the needs of a person in trouble.

But, he says, if you go out of your way to help when such injustice is done, kneel down next to the man, pick him up, put him in a taxi and take him to the hospital, even offer to pay his hospital bills, then you are a good neighbor. Your neighbors are those who are in need. There are, in other words—since we cannot encompass the whole world, and only feebly serve needs where we are—there are certain times and certain places when some people are being attacked in a way that is out of the ordinary; who are being mugged and robbed and left for dead—or hoped-for death; when the victims of injustice cry out for help. There are times when the cries of moral outrage are so intense that no one can miss them. They can be heard 'round the world. Then no matter how we would cup our hands over our ears we hear their cry for help. No matter how far on the other side of the road we would like to go, we cannot help seeing them out of the corner of our eye. And no matter how much we would like not to be troubled, we cannot stand ourselves if we do not cross over in some way to be of help—even if it be no more than to stand beside those who are robbed and outraged and join our voices to theirs.

Such a time I believe is now. The cries for help come from our Jewish friends who have been set upon, warred against on their most holy of holy days, beaten, left for a hoped-for death. The least we can do is to join our voices in protest against the killing and invasion; in protest also against powers that have within their power the power to halt hostilities.

The cry for help comes from the Jericho Road, and it is voiced by Jews throughout the world and certainly in our own city.

I referred last week to the General Convention of the Episcopal Church and its failure to take any stand of significance with regard to the Arab-Israeli conflict—what seemed to me anyway an entirely inadequate response to a cry for help. The church in effect deplored the outbreak and hoped the United Nations would stop it. It refused to distinguish between those who violated the cease-fire and those who did not. It issued nothing more than a pious hope—which every intelligent adult in the world knows is fruitless at such a time as this, unless Russia and the United States support it—that the United Nations might settle the dispute itself. The Episcopal Church passed by on the other side, and now apparently the executive committee of the National Council of Churches has done precisely the same thing with its utterly innocuous statement this past week deploring the outbreak of hostilities and hoping that the nations would resolve their differences.

The church of Christ, which teaches and preaches the parable of the Good Samaritan, has in my judgment these past two weeks distinguished itself by failing to practice what it preaches. Of course there is blame on both sides. Of course it is ambiguous and complicated. Of course the Six-Day War did not resolve the crisis—and may have added to it. But the fact is that whatever is true about the past, this war did not have to break out again in this way and it promises no end to hostilities, whatever happens on the battlefield. It is terribly complicated, very ambiguous morally, a situation which arises, as we heard this morning (in the Book of Exodus 5), out of centuries of conflict and turmoil.

But the present is what we have to deal with—it is all we have to deal with—and it is possible to act so that each step from the present into the future brings greater rather than less hope to mankind.

The church can at least say two wrongs never make a right. The church can at least stay on that side of the road where the trouble is and not walk by on the other side for fear that her own internal life might become too divided and bruised. The church can at least plead that the two great powers that have the power guarantee the borders of the Promised Land. The church can at least help bind up the wounds of those who suffer on both sides. She can do all she can to effect reconciliation. The worst she can do is to continue to pretend and to walk by on the other side.

She cannot do that and remain the church of Christ, a church sent to serve mankind in the community of mankind. That community is the only community to which we belong. We proclaim to the world that Christ is the head of that community—and his members are in pain. So may we minister to him. Amen.

Let us pray:

O God of History, Lord of Lords, King of Kings—you came to bring peace when there was war. You came to promise justice when there was injustice. We believe that you are still Lord of Lords and King of Kings, and we thank you that your peace and your justice can be brought about only by your children. Give us therefore the courage to stand for the right as you give us to see that right. Give us the humble heart to give compassion to those who are in need, and grant that we may be unafraid to declare our allegiance to you and to act in accordance with it and with the will of your Son, the King of Peace for all mankind. Amen.

Thanksgiving Day —
Day of Pain and Joy
Every Day

—∽∾—

The Twenty-second Sunday after Trinity,
November 18, 1973

The text is the phrase with which the service was opened: "This is the day which the Lord hath made; let us rejoice and be glad in it." The theme of the sermon is this: since pain and joy in our lives are inextricably bound together always, we can—if we will—make every day a Thanksgiving Day.

The sermon is of course in part prompted by the calendar. Thanksgiving Day is proclaimed by the President of the United States to be a national Thanksgiving Day—a day when the nation is undergoing pain such as she has not suffered since the Civil War.* And the President is right to make such a proclamation: the very first Thanksgiving Day was a day of great pain; and it was out of the pain of suffering, famine, and failure of nerve on the part of many that thanksgiving was given. The fact that that little, beleaguered company of Pilgrims who had made a covenant with one another under God endured the pain was sufficient cause for thanksgiving. The sufficient cause for our thanksgiving is that our nation has endured the shaking of the foundations of her national life. That is properly therefore a cause for thanksgiving today.

Without in any way condoning wrongdoing on the part of any of the leaders of our nation, we can rejoice that by and large the citizenry, in

---

*The nation was without a vice president in the wake of the resignation of Spiro T. Agnew amid criminal charges of extortion and tax evasion.

general, and great numbers of national leaders, in particular, have continued, despite the pain, to act responsibly and with integrity and to carry out the work which they have been given with courage. The fabric of our national life is not going to disintegrate. The spirit of the people of this nation bound together in a covenant under God is not going to be destroyed. And the greatness we have known in the past can be recaptured as we remain faithful to our responsibilities and as, out of the pain and suffering, a new sense of purpose and direction for the whole world is discerned—not as we direct the world but as we permit our nation to bring its strength to the brotherhood of nations.

We can, if we will and if we work, rejoice in the day because the Lord made it. To rejoice is not to lose hope, not to give up, not to turn our back upon the political life, not to turn our back upon our own responsibilities—but to give thanks for what we have and what we are, to face the truth in our national life, however unpleasant that may be, and to go forward. God has not, in his Providence, let this nation come this far under him without leading us now into paths of justice and righteousness. If we will be just and follow the right as God gives us to understand the right, this Day of Thanksgiving may be one for us to rejoice and be glad in. So, as Americans, may we with courage and enthusiasm be able to say to one another, "Happy Thanksgiving."

So the sermon is prompted in part by this national holiday, but there is another dimension to Thanksgiving Day which is deeper, more personal, and provides the source out of which all thanksgivings, including national ones, ultimately rise. It is the personal, painful experiences of life, particularly in those relationships that are nurtured by love and friendship, which emerge, mature, and grow out of pain into experiences of joy, out of suffering into infinite satisfactions, out of troubles into great strength. Those are the experiences of thanksgiving.

Pain usually comes when we cannot get our way, or when relationships are strained or broken. Friendships, for example, cease for one reason or another—a misunderstanding or an argument—and there is pain because of that broken relationship. Then one friend says to another, "Oh, come on, for heaven sakes, this is foolish. I'm sorry if it's my fault. Let's be friends again." That is the threshold of joy: the pain of separation overcome by the gladness of reunion.

A grandfather—loved, respected, noble—dies. His grandchildren act as pallbearers. After the service the family has what can only be called a celebration of joy, brought on by the departure of one who bore love to that family. It is in the breaking of that relationship that there comes a renewed, spontaneous expression of joy, deeper love for one another.

Or a young loved one dies, and here is the mystery: everyone in the family is drawn closer together than ever before. What must the Kennedy family be going through this weekend?* How they must be drawn together because of the pain of that twelve-year-old boy—the great mystery of how life is enriched and never the same again when there has been tragedy and bereavement. Bereavement, interestingly enough, is the deepest initiation into the most profound mystery of life, love, and human existence.

You can no doubt draw upon your own experiences. What are those experiences from which you have derived the greatest joy? Have they not, almost always, been associated with pain, or suffering, or dislocation, or unhappiness? A child is born, and you rejoice because the pain has gone. Without the pain and the anxiety and the worry, no joy. A difficult task you had in your life and you persevered, and because you persevered, satisfaction came—the satisfaction that was infinitely deeper than any other had you turned away from your responsibilities. An unpleasant duty is carried out, and inner strength comes to you. You are tested beyond belief to hold yourself together, and you find that you have the strength to be held together. An unjustified rebuff accepted with some measure of humility and the healing that follows. The anger that you refused to express and the grace that in time melted it. The self-pity you refused to dwell upon and the going out, the leading to new friendships, the getting on with life, the refusal to be obsessed by your feeling sorry for yourself. All these experiences, mysteriously bound together. Very seldom is there unadulterated joy. We are surprised by joy when we don't expect it because life has been so painful. That is the joy and gladness that endures.

Do you remember those words of William Blake and do they strike a chord in your memory?

> Man was made for joy and woe;
> And, when this we rightly know,
> Safely through the world we go.
> Joy and woe are woven fine,

---

*Edward M. Kennedy, Jr., the son of the senator from Massachusetts, had just had his leg amputated.

A clothing for the soul divine.

("Auguries of Innocence")

One final word. It is to go back to the text again: "This is the day which the Lord hath made; we will rejoice and be glad in it." If the day is the Lord's, if he is in it, and in everything in it—in every task, every pain, every betrayal, every suffering, every hurt, every relationship, every person, every single bit of the day—if he is in that day, then we can rejoice and be glad in it. If he is in it and we are in it, what else can we do but rejoice?

So the question is: *Is* he? Did he make this day? Is he there in whatever pain you are bearing now? Is he there in that person you can't stand? In that work you wish you didn't have to do—but you have to, and you will? In that responsibility you wish you did not have, but you have it? Is he there?

You decide, "Yes" or "No"—that is the great mystery: *you* are the one who decides. You cannot perhaps do anything about the day itself. You cannot affect in any significant way the events of the day by your decisions. You cannot straighten out any of the people you are surrounded with in that day. But what you can do is decide that this is the Lord's day, that he made it, that he is in it, that he is through everything in it.

You may not be able to change anything—except yourself and your attitude toward the day. If you decide "Yes," you bring the Lord to it. And if the Lord is in the day and you are responding to the Lord in it, then he will change it and you don't have to worry about it. Make it the Lord's day. If you do—with everything you do, with everyone you touch, with every suffering and every pain, particularly the suffering and the pain that you have—you cannot help but be helped by him, to rejoice and be glad in it.

Thanksgiving Day—Day of Pain and Joy—Every Day. "This is the day which the Lord hath made; let us rejoice and be glad in it."

Happy Thanksgiving every day! Amen.

Let us pray:

God, how did you come to make us for joy and woe, how through this world would you have us go? Joy from you and woe in you are woven fine, a clothing for our souls divine. May we therefore offer to you our woes and receive from you our joys, That day by day we may grow in your grace divine and help you make the day your own. Amen.

Our Brother Paul:
Consciousness Raising—
Christian Paradox

—ṃ—

The First Sunday in Lent,
March 3, 1974

This is the first in the Lenten series of sermons on *Our Brother Paul.* The aim of the series is to try to introduce us to his way of reflecting about the experiences of his life as a Christian in order that we may be helped to reflect intelligently about our experiences.

His experiences and ours—despite the cultural differences and the distance of years—are nevertheless very much the same. They are common, ordinary, finite, human experiences—and therefore we can properly call him "brother." When we think of Jesus Christ, we tend to call him Lord, or Savior, or Son of God, or uniquely divine—or in some way distinguishing his life and the quality of his unique being from ours. But not with Paul. He was a straightforward sinner like the rest of us. He may have been brighter—he was certainly one of the great intellects of western culture—but the stuff and the nature of his life was very much like ours—perfectly human. So we call him *Our Brother Paul.*

How did Paul, our brother, think about his life that may help us think about our lives? Paul was pre-eminently what we would call today a consciousness raiser. He was a raiser of Christian consciousness. He said, "If you are a Christian, then you should think Christianly. You should be able to affirm what it is to be a Christian, and you ought to be able to see in what goes on around you those elements which reflect the Christian understanding of human existence."

If you can begin to think about your Christian existence the way Paul does, you will not be able to help but have your Christian consciousness raised. A woman who has had her consciousness raised does not apologize for looking on life as a woman. If she is not treated properly as a woman, she lets you know about it. She is enabled to regard life from a woman's point of view and, therefore, be more of a person as a woman.

So if we are Christians, we ought to be able to look upon life as Christians, to enter into all the experiences of our life distinctively as Christians—from birth to death—and to begin to interpret everything that goes on around us from a Christian point of view. The eyes with which we behold existence are meant to be eyes of faith that are Christian.

A case in point is St. Paul's Epistle that was read this morning. How do Christians express the truth of God? Well, he says, the truth of God is expressed by Christians "By honor and dishonor, by evil report and good report: as deceivers, and *yet true;* As unknown, and yet well known; as dying and, behold, we live; as chastened, and not killed; As sorrowful, yet always rejoicing; as poor, yet making many rich; as having nothing, and *yet* possessing all things" (II Corinthians 6: 8–10). In other words, what is true in Christian experience can be expressed only by Christian paradox; that is, by seemingly contradictory statements or by statements that are so contrary to reason that they seem ludicrous. By honor and dishonor—how can it be both? As deceivers, yet true. As unknown, and yet well known. Only as these apparently contradictory statements are held together in the experience of men and women who are Christians, can the truth of the Christian faith, and therefore of their existence, be expressed.

For example, he says if you want to be a mature, responsible adult, and to put away childish things, it is necessary for you to take responsibility for the decisions of your life and then to live with those decisions. That is to be mature. Not to be a leaf tossed by the wind, not to have somebody else make your decisions for you, but to make your own decisions. Accept the responsibility for your own life. Then abide by those decisions, have the courage of your convictions—that is to act as a mature human being. You do that—and this is the other side of the paradox— *you* do that because that is *God's* doing. You work out your salvation because it is God who wills and works his way in you.

It causes you to wonder a little bit, doesn't it, about what there has been in your own experience? What there has been that has not been you, but has seemed somehow to shape you, direct you, something that seems at times to have impelled you to make certain decisions and perform certain actions, something that has been around you that has caused you at times to move ahead when you haven't had the slightest idea what the right thing to do was; but you had to make some decision and you went ahead and you did it. You acted in blind faith. Or where you have perhaps at one time or another really laid your life on the line for somebody else or for your own integrity; where you said, "No longer am I going to go along to get ahead." Why did you say that? *God* is why.

Or again he says, "I have been crucified with Christ; it is no longer I who live, but Christ who lives in me" (Galatians 2:20). It makes you think, doesn't it, about your life and the experiences you can have—when the tragedy which came to you was so powerful that it simply engulfed you and you felt you could not possibly go on; or the pain was so overwhelming that the only thing you could do was scream; or the desolation was so dark that there was no light anywhere; or the loss of someone you loved was so tremendous that you died, and you knew that you would never be the same again. And you weren't, but you went ahead anyway. You walked in the darkness, but some light did come. The nettle was there and you decided to move into it, and out of that pain and tragedy and loss you found a new life, a richer life, a more compassionate life. You were, in Paul's words, "raised." Looking back, you said, "that experience, or those experiences, of pain and loss and bereavement and death and tragedy and failure and guilt, those worst experiences, in fact seemed to cut through all the non-essentials of my life—how much money I had, or what my belongings were, or whether I was getting ahead or whether I was comfortable. I knew at those moments that I was really in touch with bed-rock reality and somehow (particularly insofar as other people were dependent upon me and how I was going to respond), somehow I found out why I was living, and what the purpose of my being here and being steadfast was."

Moreover, you may therefore have said, "That was good. That made it possible for me at that moment to be clean and honest and courageous—and to be real. There was a kind of joy about it, in fact." That is a paradox. The paradox is that pain and joy are right together. The Cross and the Resurrection are one. When my will is crucified, when I don't get my way, is when I live. Yet that is not me, that is Christ who dwells within me. That is a paradox built into the heart of human experience. You lose what you count on and you gain everything.

Well, you see the point. Paul says all truth is paradoxical: both yes and no. It is by deceiving and being true. It is by dying that we live. It is by having nothing that we possess all things. Life is not what it seems to be externally, on the surface. It is finite, but it is not just finite. It is human, but it is not just human. It is ideal, but not just ideal; you cannot live ideals. It is eternal, but not just eternal; we live in time. It is divine, but not just divine because we live naturally. It is a mixture—God and man together, the eternal and the human mixed-up. The divine breaking into our nature. Reason and faith, mixed, to give us a perspective and a power.

Life always more than it seems, tragedy never the last word. Hope is the last word in all things, Paul says. *All* things—hope, richness, joy. Crazy, isn't it? Really just ridiculous. All things work together for good—well, yes and no. Some things are terrible. All things work together for good to them *who love God.*

Even in worship, he says, even in congregations, gathered together, your worship is meant to be such—intelligent, reasonable, sincere—that when a stranger comes in he should be able to say, "God really is in your midst."

So if a stranger comes in, and looks around, he is aware, certainly, of human frailty. He recognizes our human selfishness and sin, our hankering after things we don't have, wanting more than we have, searching for things to find our security. But if he has eyes to see, and a spirit by which to be sensitive to people, he sees also hope, infinite courage, steadfastness, quietly holding on, compassion, concern, love, loyalty, longing, yearning for the best and the highest. If he comes with a sensitive spirit and with eyes that are open to what is going on in this service of worship he is in touch with the spirit of worship in truth and in grace and he can say, "God really is here in your midst." The paradox is that through us, just ordinary human beings, God is made visible.

In this particular service of the Holy Communion we have that paradoxical center where there is just some ordinary bread and some ordinary wine. When we offer those in thanksgiving to God for Christ and what he has done for us in the experiences of our lives, and we offer those experiences and ourselves to him, then lo and behold!—the bread and the wine become his body and blood. Ridiculous, isn't it? But that is the way God is, in Christ. Those symbols become the power of God for our life, so that we can live with hope and strength and joy. The paradox: bread and wine become Christ.

No matter, therefore, what your life seems to be, how forlorn or difficult, how trying the circumstances, how heavy the cares, how tragic the vision, raise your consciousness Christianly. This is also Christ's life. Everything in your life is [Christ's], and he is raising you to a new life of hope and power and joy.

That is a paradox, a Christian paradox, and it is the truth. So let your consciousness be raised so that you may not only be able to see him in your life, but as you participate in his offering, share him, and then, of course, live him. Amen.

On Riding Motorcycles

——∿——

The Fifteenth Sunday after Trinity, September 22, 1974

One of the happiest memories of my childhood, which on the whole was a happy one, is of motorcycle rides. A young man in our neighborhood owned a motorcycle, and on summer evenings he would stop by the porch where I frequently was with other members of our family, and he would say "want a ride?" Would I! And finally, with my parents' permission—a debate each time he asked the question—he would lift me, aged four or five years old, on to the saddle; he sat behind me, put his hands on the handle bars, locking me safely in, turn the throttle, race the motor, and off we would go in a cloud of dust! We bent dangerously as we went around the corners at a thousand miles an hour; we went like the wind, and as Tom Swift used to say "the motorcycle ate up the road."

Exciting and exhilarating! Nothing quite like it. The words: *"Harley Davidson"*—noble words that lifted one's heart just as much as the words at that time, *Babe Ruth, Yankee Stadium,* and *Lou Gehrig!*

That dream of owning a motorcycle finally came true during freshman year at college when my roommate and I bought a second-hand motorcycle in Philadelphia for twenty-five dollars. We had to forge the name of a friend, because it was against the rule for undergraduates in those olden days to have motorcycles or automobiles. We forged his name with his permission because we were going to store the motorcycle in his barn.

That drive from Philadelphia, that sense of ecstasy and freedom, what Toad in *The Wind in the Willows* called "the thrill of the open road," was all that we had anticipated and more. For several weeks we would hitchhike out to Hopewell where we kept that motorcycle and we would then spin around the countryside exalting in life as only college freshmen can, especially when there is also the thrill of knowing you are breaking the law—and getting away with it!

One Sunday afternoon the motorcycle broke down. We had not the slightest idea how to put it together again, nor to care for it, nor, I suppose, really the desire to learn how to take care of the motorcycle. It was too technical a proposition for us—we concentrated on Latin Poets in those days. No garage was open so we pushed the motorcycle those four or five miles from Lawrenceville to Hopewell, sold it the following week for twenty-five dollars, and I haven't been on a motorcycle since.

Now, I mention this fascinating data of my autobiography in order to establish my credibility as a commentator upon the book, *Zen and the Art of Motorcycle Maintenance* by R. M. Pirsig which I read this summer and which I commend to you. It is one of the most interesting, unusual, profound discussions of the world of ideas and of values that I have ever read. It is in my judgment an absolute tour de force, wherein he takes the concepts of knowledge, self-knowledge, right and wrong, meaning, and puts those traditional disciplines in an absolutely fresh way. Without using any of the traditional religious words, it is in fact as religious a book as I have read in a long time and certainly infinitely more interesting than most religious books.

So, *Zen and the Art of Motorcycle Maintenance.* The author, a college professor, middle-aged, lost his job. Riding his motorcycle through the Northwest from Montana to the Pacific Coast and on the back seat is his teenaged son. Sometimes that relationship is warm and friendly, mutually understanding and supportive, sympathetic; at other times it's broken, they are estranged, alienated, do not understand each other, hurt each other.

The father himself has been alienated within himself. He has had a breakdown and been in a mental hospital, and tries to understand that thin line between rationality and irrationality. He is a motorcycle buff, knows everything about motorcycles, loves his motorcycle, loves to keep the engine in perfect tune. He describes in a fascinating way how a motorcycle is put together, the different parts, how they all have a special place, how a rider can keep that motorcycle functioning well, up over the mountains and down through the valleys, over the desert. What a personal caring relationship is established between a rider who loves his motorcycle and the motorcycle.

So it's a story, a travel diary. He tells about his trip from day to day and interspersed are a series of reflections about his journey and what that journey means to him. It is, of course, a symbol of his journey through life—of every man's journey—yours and mine—starting somewhere, ending somewhere. He reflects upon what it means and his understanding, what its purpose is. He loves the riding, just the riding. "Sometimes," he writes (trying to describe that deep sense of satisfaction in the riding when everything is all right with the person behind him), "sometimes it's a little better to travel than to arrive." In urging us therefore to accept the reality of the present and to take it all in just as much as we are able to, he comments that when you want to hurry, "when you want to hurry something, that means that you no longer care about it and you want to get on with other things." So he talks about caring, right now, for what you are doing right now. Spend your energy on the present, don't agonize about hoping to get the goal tomorrow; those goals don't come. The goal is in the riding, the present.

Caring, he says, is everything and caring means, amongst other things, caring for the maintenance of your motorcycle. So the motorcycle is also a symbol. It's a symbol of our modern technological society. It is the symbol of the end result of Greek thought and Roman thought and Western culture where reason has developed essentially a scientific, secular understanding of nature, where science has harnessed nature, exploited nature and may yet be destroyed by it. Pollution, for example, the by-product of our scientific age, may yet spell the end of that culture. In any case, the motorcycle is a small, easily understood machine. (If I had had his book in Lawrenceville, I might have been able to put it back together again.)

He uses as the symbol of man's rational nature in that world of ideas the motorcycle, the exercise of the intellect which has resulted in our technological society. Sometimes it's referred to as the right hand that man has of grasping, thinking, balancing pros and cons, judging, the expression of his reason. He maintains that at its best that Greek/Roman/Western scientific thought had been concerned essentially about *Quality*. Rational man has, at his best, always wanted to do a quality job. Whether it is the world of ideas reflecting the quality of perfect ideas in Plato, or whether it's building a quality road, or developing a quality culture, or building a quality atomic reactor, or making and keeping the motorcycle in terms of its best quality—that is what man uses his reason for.

The theme of the book is that man's nature is most fully expressed when this rational right-hand nature—the motorcycle—is joined with his intuitive nature, his feeling, his love nature symbolized by the boy in the back seat.

The caring that he has for his son, the caring and love he has for his journey and for the motorcycle, somehow are meant to be all of a piece. And this left-hand, intuitive, feeling, feminine side, emotional side, he says, joined together with the right-hand makes the whole person. Two natures, the outer and the inner, are two aspects of the same thing. A person who *sees* quality and also *feels* it as he works, is a person who cares. A person who cares about what he sees and does is a person who is bound to have some characteristics of quality.

Do you want to live a life of quality? Well one way is to care. *Caring and Quality* then emerge as the marks of the whole person. Finally, there emerges what the book is about. "The real cycle you're working on," he writes, "is a cycle called yourself. The machine that appears to be "out there" and the person who appears to be "in here" are not two separate things. They grow toward quality or fall away from quality, together."

I have taken the time to describe this book at such length not only to suggest that you read it (if you are interested in the world of ideas you will be fascinated by it) but also because it seems to me to present precisely what the Christian Faith is about in non-religious terms (and in a somewhat distorted way what the Christian Church is about). It's describing a journey, outward and inward, where caring and quality are the essential ingredients. The biblical words are Love and Truth—lived most fully by Jesus who was filled with Love and Truth and who said: I am the Way and the Truth. The goal is a life lived truthfully and lovingly and it's lived *now*. We are not to worry, drive desperately toward the end of the journey; the end and the way are the same; our journey is meant to be as satisfying and whole as possible; we are meant in that journey to reflect our whole nature, our emotional as well as our rational. Our head and our heart are meant to go together and the songs that we sing with our hearts are meant to make sense to our heads, as we care for one another and for ourselves.

The real cycle we are always working on is ourselves and as we journey caring we always grow toward quality—toward Christ. As we grow toward him on our journey we can remember he is the Way. It's not simply *our* journey we are taking, it is *his* as well. It's his right now. He won't let us fall off, because his hands are on the handle bars and the cycle he is working on is ourselves, caring for us that we may care and so become quality people—sheer quality, wholly ourselves in Love and in Truth.

Jesus, we can't keep our balance without you. We can't go anywhere, be anybody without you. So you be our guide now on our Journey. You drive. Let us rejoice in just the day we have, as we set out once more for this day's journey. Let us rejoice in everything and everyone just as they are, caring for them as you do, and loving ourselves as you do. Help us be whole persons growing toward holiness and the safe journey's end in you. Amen.

Justice and Mercy

—∿—

The Feast of St. Michael and All Angels, September 29, 1974

Let me begin this morning by asking you to exercise your imagination. Imagine a courtroom scene where there is a trial taking place. On the bench is the judge. His task is to so understand what the law says that he may apply it to the case at hand in the light of the facts that are presented so that justice may prevail. On one side there is the prosecuting attorney, and on the other, the defense attorney. Their task is to use the law as skillfully as they can so that the accused may be, on the one hand, determined guilty or on the other, innocent.

Then there is the accused—accused, let us say, of stealing $5,000 from his employer. And in order that you might have a real exercise of your imagination, imagine that you are the prisoner. You stand accused of this crime violating the laws of the land. (Now you may prefer some other crime, so let your imagination roam for a moment and think of any crime you would really like to commit. What would you really like to do in violation of the law?)

Now, let us suppose in this imaginary courtroom scene that, whatever the crime, you are innocent. No matter how damaging the circumstantial evidence is as it begins to mount, you know that even if you are convicted, you are in fact innocent. You can't be shaken in that knowledge. You have an absolute inner confidence in your own innocence, and you know that when all the truth is out, everyone will know you are innocent.

Suppose, then, that before all the evidence in this courtroom scene is in, before, in fact, you have even been called to testify in your own behalf, the judge asks if you would be interested in having a mistrial declared so that he can set you free. He promises you by whatever legal device would be at hand to pardon you. What would you do? Would you accept that pardon that was offered? Or would you ask him to complete the trial? If you are innocent, do you want the facts to come out so that justice can prevail, or not? That is the first scene I ask you to think of in your imagination.

Now the second. The setting is exactly the same—the judge, once a lawyer trying to use the law for the sake of his clients, now trying to determine what the law itself says so he can be used by the law to interpret it. The lawyers on either side presenting the best case they can to prosecute or to defend. Again you are the prisoner, but this time you are guilty. (What was that crime that your imagination a moment ago tempted you to commit? Well, you did it, and now you're before the judge, and you're guilty. You know it, but at the moment, nobody else knows it.) Then the judge says, "Would you be interested at this juncture in a mistrial, so you can go free? You can, in effect, be pardoned." What would you say? If you are guilty, do you want the facts to come out so that justice can prevail, or not?

Now in a moment, the third and last act of imagination. You understand, I trust, by now that these imaginative reconstructions of trials do, in fact, reveal a reality about existence, your existence and mine. Whether in any particular incident we are innocent or guilty, we are always innocent or guilty in relationship to the law, in relationship to right or wrong, in relationship to a set of values determined by society or to codes of behavior. So, as we journey through life, we always make this pilgrimage of innocence and guilt in relationship to a law that stands above us and that judges us. Sometimes we are innocent; sometimes we are guilty. But we always are under the law that judges us. And when we are judged, maybe there is the judge on the bench in a courtroom that judges us; or maybe the judge that we carry with us all our life long is our parents. They first exposed us to judgment, and we've never been able to get free of searching for their approval—or in some contrary instances always doing that which we know they will disapprove of just because that's who they are and who we are. Or maybe the judge is the social group to which we belong, and we say with regard to our behavior, "Well, what would people think?" Or maybe the judge is not in our set but in another set to which we aspire, and we're trying to get approval from that group. "How can I impress them with my behavior so they will accept me and let me in?"

Well, in any case, there is always this kind of external judgment pronouncing us innocent or guilty, and along with that external judgment, there is always the internal judge. That internal judge is oneself. Whether I am innocent or guilty, no matter what, I always have to live with myself. In other words, judgment and justice are an inevitable part of life—built right into it from the beginning to the end.

So the third scene. The judge again puts himself under the law so he might execute the law. The lawyers present the best case they can make in light of the facts and the law. And you, the accused. You are guilty this time, too. Two out of three times, you're guilty—somewhat more often guilty than innocent in the course of a lifetime is an accurate description of the lives of most of us. We are more guilty in our lives than we are innocent. When we have to describe ourselves in the terms we have been using this morning, and think of ourselves in relationship to judgment, we pronounce ourselves guilty because we are not the persons we know we are meant to be—regardless of how many overt acts of violation of the law we have committed.

The biblical word for this is that we have "Fallen," that is, we're more concerned about ourselves than we are about anybody else in the world. The fullest expression of this is found in our pride. We set ourselves, or we are tempted to set ourselves, over against other people so we are doing the judging. And we are tempted to judge them in accordance with what we believe is right for ourselves. ("He doesn't amount to much!" "She's not so hot!" "Why don't they change their ways?") We look at life from our perspective. By our nature, our human nature, we almost always put ourselves over against or above them. Sometimes, by a special act of grace, we are able spontaneously to put ourselves sympathetically and compassionately in the position of the other person. When that happens, we understand there is a dimension to life which is beyond our own judgment and beyond our own interests. Curiously enough, when we really do that, we say, "That is the way I am meant to be as a person." But, that usually is not the day-in-and-day-out experience.

So the trial unfolds; the evidence comes in. It may be as you listen to the evidence (and you know the judge is listening), that as the evidence of what you have done and who you are comes in, you have a sense of relief. "Yes, that's true. That is the kind of person I am, and now that the judge and everybody knows it, then I don't have to cover myself up anymore and pretend to be something or someone whom I'm not."

Judgment, curiously enough, seems to lift burdens from us. Where would we be if there was no judgment in life? So, when the judge declares you guilty of having violated the law of which he is the custodian and interpreter (he doesn't own the law; it's not his judgment; it's the judgment of the law), he passes judgment, you then accept it as the truth, because he knows it and you know it. You and the law have come to terms with one another; justice is carried out in your judgment. At your best moments then, you say, "Yes, that is the way it is. Thank God!"

What then? Having this accomplished, if the judge should say, "Would you be interested in going free now? Would you accept my pardon now?" What would you say?

We are trying to get a Christian perspective on judgment. When the Christian knows he is guilty of violating the law, he knows he is violating God's law. His offence is against God as well as against society and himself. His disobedience is to his God-given nature, and he becomes less than God intends him to be. And he knows it. When you stand in the prisoner's dock, and you know you are known by him, "unto whom all hearts are open and all desires known," as a Christian you also know, don't you, that the judge on the bench is Christ. He is the interpreter of the divine law. He knows the mind and the heart of the giver of the laws of justice, just as he knows your heart and mind and mine. And when he pronounces judgment, he does no more than reveal and pronounce God's truth about you.

But when Christ is the judge and pronounces judgment, he then comes down from the bench and says, "I'm going to take your place. You go free. You are pardoned. You are forgiven. Go live your life as a free man." He sets us free from our sins. He sets us free of our guilt. He sets us free to live out the glorious liberty of the children of God. *He* does it; we don't. All we do is to confess the truth about ourselves. He then reveals the truth about God. God is a God of justice and of mercy, not one or the other, but both together. He loves us so much that he won't let us get away with anything in violation of our true natures. He loves us so much that he will give us that which we can never provide—forgiveness and mercy all the days of our lives. That's a gift from him. We can't earn it. We don't deserve it. It's unconditional. Absolution. That's God.

Well, this is a parable. A parable is a story about life told from a Christian perspective describing God—in Christ—in our lives. We are meant to look at all the events of life—the personal events, the social events, the national events—from something of that perspective. Christ, and all that is caught up in him, all that's caught up in that story of the Christian faith, the revealing of the nature and the mystery of the heart and mind of God, enables us to be lifted at least a little bit above the ordinary perspective of human justice, revenge, partisanship, self-will. The prosaic and the passions of the self are meant to be left a little bit behind so we can look at the scene and participate in it with a meaning that comes from beyond us—looking at our existence a little bit from his point of view.

So, we are not meant, when we translate that scene into the political realm or the national realm, as Christians, to be in agreement on one point of view about the trials we go through in life or that our nation goes through. But we are meant to be both observing and participating in those trials every day of our lives as Christian men and women, acting in them as people who know the judge is Christ, who is also our Savior—the one who sets us free—judge and Savior together. Not one or the other. No conditions except acceptance of the truth, ourselves, and of him.

Well, like all parables, the story has to be lived out in the story of every person's life. You will live out that story as you are able in the story of your life. So if your judge says to you now at the end of this imaginative series of trials, "Do you want to be free? Do you want to be free to go be yourself?" How would you respond? Would you let him take your place? Do you want him to?

The end of the story is, if you want him to, he will take your place. He has already, in fact, done so. So go in peace. The Lord has put away your sins. You are free.

God, don't let our conscience be our guide, alone, because our self-will so often determines the voice of our conscience. Rather, let our conscience be guided by you— guided into the ways of justice and mercy so that we may be just and merciful because of your indwelling presence and the gift of the guidance and the life of your son, our judge, our savior who sets us free. Amen.

Creative Christian Conflict

—⚏—

The Seventeenth Sunday after Trinity, October 6, 1974

In following this sermon, you may be helped by turning to the Epistle that has just been read because that is the text. It is on page 213 in the Prayer Book. [*Editor's note: The text is from Ephesians 4:1–6, as rendered in the 1928 version of the Book of Common Prayer: "I therefore, the prisoner of the Lord, beseech you that ye walk worthy of the vocation wherewith ye are called, with all lowliness and meekness, with long-suffering, forbearing one another in love; endeavouring to keep the unity of the Spirit in the bond of peace. There is one body, and one Spirit, even as ye are called in one hope of your calling; one Lord, one faith, one baptism, one God and Father of all, who is above all, and through all, and in you all."*]

While you are finding the place, I might tell you what has prompted this sermon. It is what has come to be known as "the Philadelphia incident," when three retired bishops of the Episcopal Church this summer laid their hands on eleven women deacons and declared them ordained in the church of God as priests—in defiance of the position of the Episcopal Church taken at the General Convention in Louisville a year ago. Those bishops and those deacons acted in good conscience in response to what they believed to be the call of God. Other members of the church have disagreed with their action because of their equally conscientious conviction that that action was not in accord with God's will as it is known in this church.

The sermon is prompted by this incident, but you will probably be relieved to know that it is not going to be the subject of the sermon—

the ordination of women to the priesthood. That belongs elsewhere at another time, or if here, not this morning. What it prompts, of course, is this question of conscientious conflict. What do you do when you are in disagreement with someone whose conscience you respect but whose judgment you question? What do you do when you belong to an institution and profess loyalty to that institution whose laws you believe you should not—in accordance with your own conscience, in obedience to your conscience—obey?

You have, have you not, had disagreements with people or quarrels with institutions to which you belong on this level? This is not simply an argument over whether someone else is going to get his way. That is simply a struggle of the ego. You want to overpower somebody with your arguments. This is infinitely deeper than that because the disagreement arises out of a bond or a fellowship or a relationship that is one of trust, sometimes of love, and you and another find yourselves in conscientious disagreement. Then what do you do? If your experience is anything like mine, faced with that kind of conflict, you have perhaps frequently quieted your conscience, not had the moral courage to obey it and gone on less of a person than you were. At least that's been my experience.

So this sermon is about conflict in that sense, and on an even deeper level, conflict in a Christian sense. Its title is *Creative Christian Conflict*. What are we meant to do when we are bound to one another, or want to be bound to one another, in love, when we really care for one another because we are bound in our different ways to God in a fellowship, a trust? What does God's involvement in our disagreement mean? When we are fundamentally in deep conscientious conflict, and we know that we have to oppose one another in love, how does God make any difference?

Well, that's what the text is about. It's not about how you settle arguments with your neighbor in the apartment next door who keeps his record player too high too late at night; nor does it have to do with the arguments you have with a taxi driver who hits your fender; nor even the arguments you have with your employer who tells you what to do and you don't like it. It is about disagreements, arguments, conflicts, battles with people and institutions whom you love, and whom you know God loves just as much as you do. Or people, to use a Biblical phrase, or people whom you love "in Christ."

Here is the translation of the text. It is a free translation, and it's mine. It may not fit your situation, in which case you'll have to make your own translation. In fact, you'll have to make your own anyway. So this will be an illustration.

I'm asking you now. I am begging you now. I am imploring you now. I'm not telling you. I'm not ordering you. I'm not commanding you. I don't have any right to do that, nor to impose myself or my understanding upon you. Nobody can make you do anything, except as you feel compelled by God himself to do something. I can ask you to do something, as I ask myself, only because we both belong to God. And I can bear witness, as I am able and have the courage to, to my own understanding of God's will. I say, in fact, to put it as sharply as possible, I say I am a 'prisoner of God.' I am locked into him. I can't do anything significantly except be in accordance with him. I can't even budge except I act in accordance with his Spirit, and neither can you, because you believe you belong to him in reality in exactly the same way.

Of course, we all know we don't always act this way. We tend to make decisions as if we were absolutely free to do what we wanted to with our lives. We set our hearts on goals that we think are important, without any reference to his will. We say that the real meaning of our lives is going to be found in the money we earn, or the positions we earn or are given to us, or the prestige that we have, or the sexual freedom we demand, or whatever. We act as if we were free agents, but down deep we know we're not free agents. Down deep we know that all of that external goal setting and commitment to those external goals—all that is rubbish. The real meaning of our lives is never, never found in our estate planning, or in the positions we attain, or the honors that are given to us, or the bodily satisfactions and fulfillments of life. They are all part of life. They all can be very good, but never do they ever carry ultimate meaning. In the long run, when those are our final goals, they're rubbish. We can't—however desirable and proper they may be—we can't afford to become prisoners of them. We're prisoners of the Lord. When we do our best to obey him, and what he wants as our goal, then strangely enough we are most free. And strangely enough, it is there that we have our enduring satisfactions.

So what we want in our common relationship, what you and I want in our common relationship, is to be able to set each other free, to help each other serve the Lord whose prisoner each one is. In other words, I want to help you do what you conscientiously believe God wants you to do. That's your vocation. That is your calling—to respond to him as fully as you can, to do what he wants. I want to help you follow that vocation with all my power, as I hope you want to help me follow my vocation.

Now to do that, we have to listen to each other, really listen. We can't move in to straighten anybody else out. We can't be too certain of our own understanding of God's will. We have to be a little humble about our pretentions to know what God wants. My conscience never can be formed all by itself. To say that I'm going to let my conscience be my guide is as arrogant a statement as I can make, because then I have decided what God wants me to do. It's got to be God who decides. So my conscience is going to be formed in part by your conscience and your judgment. When I love you, and you know it, you will then speak to me because you will know that I am not trying to remake you into anything except what our common Lord wants for you. Our consciences are to be guided by one another and by him who is the Lord of both. And when we listen to one another, when we listen to one another caring for one another, we are more apt to come to a common mind and conscience than in any other way. Most divisions in life occur because we want our way and want to impose it on others. We don't really want his way. His comes when we are genuinely willing to hang in there, to listen to one another, because that's the only way we can ever hear him.

That is called trying to keep the unity of the Spirit. It is not the unity of an institution that is important. It's the unity of the Spirit. And sometimes the only way the unity of the Spirit can be maintained is to let the institution go, or at least let it be broken and then be reformed more in accordance with his Spirit. To have our hearts set upon the unity of an institution as the goal of life is no better Christianly than to have our hearts set upon the money we put in the bank. The Spirit is one, and when people are in the Spirit, they are one. They are one in the Spirit even though they may have vast differences of opinion.

That being one in the Spirit is the bond of peace. The bond of peace doesn't mean that everyone is in agreement. It means that everyone is one in the Spirit. If everyone is in agreement all the time, it is a pretty good sign that agreement is around something other than the Spirit—like "let's not rock the boat," "let's keep everybody together"—because the Spirit is always making new. It is always recreating, reforming, transforming people and institutions more into the likeness of our common Lord. That's what it means to be in Christ, in love, in the Spirit; helping those you love to be recreated, continually being remade yourself as you share that Spirit and it lives in you.

So don't be afraid of conflict. No conflict—no gospel. Sometimes conflict is the only way we discover that in our true natures we all belong to one body, one Spirit, one faith, one baptism, one God. So when conflict comes between people, or groups of people who are bound together in the unity of the Spirit, and they're trying to help one another obey the Spirit in their differing interpretations and to trust one another, then the one Spirit prevails and probably no one person's particular interpretation of the Spirit prevails. There are times when this is the only way—through conflict—that the Spirit carries his way. This should, of course, be no surprise to those who believe that the way God broke most wholly into the world was through the breaking of his Son's body on the Cross as he obeyed his Father.

So the translation of the last clause in the text:

God is above and beyond all our conflicts, agonies, and struggles. God is God above us. God is also everywhere at all times and in all places including our conflicts, agonies, and struggles. God is God among us. God is also within us, within you and me, he is that Spirit within us calling us to be obedient to him so we can become free as we are meant to be. God is God within us. He is all in all and in him, so are we.

Amen.

Scenes From a Marriage

—⚭—

The Eighteenth Sunday after Trinity, October 13, 1974

Two scenes from the Ingmar Bergman film *Scenes from a Marriage*. In the first scene midway through the movie, the wife, Liv Ullmann, is speaking with her husband after he has returned temporarily from a trip abroad with another woman. She is trying to explain to him how she was able to begin to put her life back together again after it had been shattered by his leaving her and their two children after ten years of a purportedly very happy marriage. "The trouble with our marriage," she says, "was, from my point of view, my inability ever to find out who I was. All I ever was told to do was to please others. And so I tried to please others, especially my parents and then you, my husband." She went on, "I was determined by other people, and I can't do that anymore. I'm going to determine who I am myself. Now after this tragic shattering of my life, I have in fact begun to discover who I am and to trust myself. There are three ingredients: I have my common sense; I have my feelings; and I also have my experience. I've been able, in effect, now to come to terms with my life and with myself." She has imposed some sense of order on her life.

The second scene is the final one in the movie. That begins with the couple asleep—several years and several lovers later. The wife is suddenly awakened by a terrible nightmare; her husband wakes up, puts his arm around her and says, "Tell me, what is the trouble?" "Well," she said, "I was running, and I had my hands out to hold you and our two children, but my hands had disappeared. I had only stumps and I couldn't grab you. And I was sinking in the quagmire." So her husband with his arm around her says, "Apparently your well-ordered life can't cope with every dimension of your existence." She looks at him and says, "The trouble is I've never been able to love anyone, and no one has ever been able to love me." Then he replies, "Well, I love you in my inept, selfish way. And you love me in your dominating, demanding way. We do love each other—not perfectly, but that's the way we are."

And by implication, that's the way life is. We somehow have to come to terms with it. The way life is—no matter how we try to impose our order on it—we still have nightmares. No matter how often we run and skip with our hands joined together, there are still times when we only have stumps for arms; we reach out and we can't hold on to anybody; and we are sinking into the quagmire. No matter how we love, we never love enough. And our love for others is always intertwined with our love for ourselves. We love ineptly, selfishly, demandingly, dominatingly. That's the way our love is. That's the way we are. That's the way life is.

In fact, it is deeper than that. Life is terribly ambiguous. We are a body, live in a body, and in the body there is a spirit. We look at life with a certain kind of spirit that is more than our body. We love people, and we use them at the same time. We are loved and we are exploited at the same time. And you don't have to live very long to see that if you are going to affirm *life*, you have to deal with *death*. We rejoice in our existence—in our loves and lives and loyalties and friendships—and down deep we know that they're all going to come to an end one day. They don't last.

So in this ambiguous life, we are anxious. We're anxious to come to terms with it, with ourselves, with the ambiguities and the mixture we find within ourselves, with its exhilarations and depressions, with its glory and its tragedies, with its fulfillments and its frustrations, with its beginnings and with its endings. So as we try to come to terms with these anxieties that rise up out of life, we try to come to terms with life itself . . . with our lives. Would you listen for a moment to this description of how we do this, or at least of how one man does it?

"This man is outwardly a successful, real, honest-to-God man. He is a college graduate. He is a husband and a father. He is a good son to his parents; and now that his father has died, he continues to take his family to have Sunday dinner with his mother. He has a responsible position in his business firm, likes the routine of his work more than the work itself. After a week's vacation, he gets restless and irritable. He is glad finally when the vacation is done and he goes back to the office. So is his wife.

"His children for the most part have grown up and gone their separate ways and have chosen different styles of living. He is disappointed in them. He says to his wife that they've let him down. He probably feels deep down inside that he has let them down in ways that he doesn't understand. When his wife suggests that they all come together as members of the family to try to deal with their relationship to one another and identify the reasons for their separation, he says, 'No, I don't want any more "heart-to-hearts." They're too much.'

"Is he a Christian? Well, after his fashion, he would say that he was. But he doesn't like to talk about it. 'It's a very personal matter,' he says. 'I have my own religion.' He seldom goes to church—weddings, funerals, Christmas Eve carol service, Easter (leaves before the Communion if he can). Church makes him uneasy. He says that clergy don't really know what they're talking about because they don't know the real world the way he does and the way men of affairs do. He makes one exception in the case of one clergyman whom he likes, and of whom he concedes that he does know what he's talking about. But he doesn't want to hear him for another reason—he has a fear that this might lead him too far. He doesn't want to face too much."

Does this sound familiar? Does this describe anybody you know? You know who wrote it? Søren Kierkegaard, the Danish theologian and philosopher, in the year 1848. He is describing all of us in part—how we get our defenses up against the terrifying aspects of life, the deep anxieties and ambiguities and contradictions of our existence.

Somehow we have to deal with this mysterious paradox of who we are. With one side of our nature, we belong to the animal world. We are born, we reproduce, and we die just as everyone in the animal world does. Yet we also have a curious way of looking at this life that arises out of our minds and the spirit which we bring to examine this life. We are in nature, and we are more than nature. We are on the one hand creators—we can fly to the moon; we can also write a poem about the moonlight; we can sing songs and paint pictures; we can make love . . . spiritual love as well as physical love. We can in fact sacrifice our bodies because of our spirits and our loyalties in the spirit. We are creators—the crown of creation—and yet we are also creatures. We are also dispirited, depressed, dishonest, disoriented, defeated creatures at times. We are both creators and creatures, angels and animals, glorious and tragic, living and dying.

Both Kierkegaard and Bergman describe how therefore we tend to settle for life on a mediocre level, imposing our order upon it. No great loves, but then no great betrayals either. No lofty exaltations, but then no crushing defeats. Not much life, not all of the life we know we're meant to have, but then we're going to die anyway.

Temporizing, compromising mediocrity is one way in which we deal with this paradoxical nature of ours. It probably is the way that most of us in our secular, middle class culture try to get through life.

There are two other ways. One is that instead of trying to hold our two natures together, we try to settle for one or the other. Some people try to repudiate the spirit and to dwell on the body, to find meaning in their food or drink or sexual liaisons or material possessions—a modern form of "Let us eat, drink, and be merry, for tomorrow we die" (although it is in fact a repudiation of classical Epicureanism because it is totally selfish). The other is found in those who want to deny the body and its demands and satisfactions and requirements. They say, "we're going to express our spirit; we're going to be loyal to our spiritual nature and that pure, crystal-clear exaltation of who we are under God. We are going to live on that level and deny the body." This kind of a body/spirit split becomes what we call "schizoid." We end up breaking down; we are both body and spirit. We can no more settle for bodily satisfactions alone on the one hand, than we can jump out of our skins on the other. We have to deal with the ambiguous character of both together.

So we come to the conclusion. If we are both body and spirit—with a touch of the angel about us and more than a touch of the animal—if we are both creators of life and created by life, if we can walk around the moon and tell the moon how much we love someone and write a love sonnet—who are we that we can do these things? It is not enough to describe our ambiguous existence. What does it *mean?* If we can find the answer neither in our bodies nor in our spirit, where can we? How do you answer that question for yourself? Who are you? Where do you really belong? Where do you feel at home? Whose are you? Anybody's?

Well, those questions, of course, nobody can answer for anybody else. You can answer them for yourself as I can try to answer them for myself. Those are questions that the Jews and Christians have wrestled with ever since the dawn of history.

In the Old Testament lesson (Isaiah 6:1–8) Isaiah says, "There is the Lord, high and lifted up. He tells me to come. I want to respond to this vision of holiness, but how can I come? I am a man of unclean lips and I dwell in the midst of people of unclean lips. I want to approach holiness and I need to be cleansed to do so. Only God can do that. I can't. Man can't. Only God can. He sends the angel to burn my sins away and forgive me."

In other words, the only way I can respond to the ambiguities of life is to respond to *God*. Some One above those ambiguities.

Can you believe that? Can you say, "Yes, I can," or "I wish I could," or "I want to"? Can you say, when you come into this holiness church, I believe the Lord is here, high and lifted up? And when you go out into your other relationships—those ambiguous ones—can you say, "I sense his spirit there as well"?

If you can say something like that—"I want to trust that spirit is moving through my life and my relationships. I want to trust life a little more, to love people a little more, to affirm people a little more, care for them, provide some better kind of justice for those I cannot touch personally"—then you have decided for faith. If you can say, "At least in my best moments I am in that spirit and I trust that spirit to carry me over all the ambiguities and contradictions and broken relationships in life, including that of death"—then you have made an act of faith.

That is what Liv Ullmann and her husband were not able to say. People who are flat out in our culture, who have no vertical dimension to their lives, but who are flat out in relationship only to one another and to their bodies and their twisted spirits, cannot say that. To say it requires an act of faith, a decision that something more is going on than is visible, and to trust it.

That closing scene in the movie is utterly honest in its realism, it is quite touching in its mutual human accepting of incomplete love, of incomplete selves—but it is of course finally hopeless. An ending with hope would be, "What little love we do have, and however twisted it may be, we shall now trust to the best of our ability. We shall commit ourselves to love the spirit and each other who bear it. That is our faith. We will act on it."

The ending in life might not have been any happier, but it would have been filled with infinite hope. It comes from the God of all hope.
Amen.

God's Sense of Humor

———∽∾———

The First Sunday after Epiphany, January 12, 1975

This is the time of year when application blanks from high school seniors must be completed if they hope to get into the college of their choice—or even the college not of their choice. They fill out the application blanks and send them in with the transcript of their grades, the record of the scholastic aptitude tests that they have been taking for the past two and one-half years, and a letter of evaluation from the principal of the secondary school. Most of you undoubtedly know what a trying time this is from now until April when the acceptance and the rejection slips come in, not only for the seniors themselves but also for the parents and grandparents and for the little brothers and sisters. It is a time when clouds of paranoia tend to settle upon certain segments of our society. Grades, tests, records, relative standing in the class, evaluations by superiors, judgments—all take on an obsessive character for thousands of young people. This is the next to last step in a process that began when their parents first filled out their application for nursery school (and asked clergymen to provide references for three-year-olds; usually the more difficult the three-year-old, the more hope for him in life).

I ask you to turn your attention to another application blank this morning. Let me ask you to fill out, at least in part, an application blank for a college. It is undoubtedly the most highly competitive admissions process of any college in the country. There are 3,000 applications each year for an entering class of fifty. It asks a number of unusual questions. I am going to ask you to answer some of those questions that are taken from the application blank. It seems only fair that if I ask you the questions and ask you to answer them that I ask myself the same questions and share with you some of the answers that I give. After the normal autobiographical data has been asked and you have presented it, here is the next question.

1. "If you could be someone else, who would you be and why?"

   Is there someone that you have known in your life or some people that you have known that you would like to have been like—when you might have said, "I wish I could act like that person or express that kind of spirit or attitude. I wish I could be like that." What are your fantasies about the fullest life that you could have? Would you like to be one person or a combination of traits of people? Who would you like to be? Well, I would like to be a combination of Thomas Merton, Tom Mix, and Martin Luther King Jr.

2. "What character trait in yourself would you like most to change?"

   I would have to answer that—arrogance. How would *you* answer it? Not just the self-righteousness of clergy who professionally pretend to speak in the name of God, but personally. What is *your* worst character trait? You cannot beat that one.

3. "How do you occupy your solitary hours when you are all by yourself? What do you enjoy most doing?"

   I enjoy negotiating with God.

4. "When was the last time you cried? For what reason?"

   Well, I cried last summer for the last time on the beach just after dawn, and I cried because it was so incredibly beautiful, and I just could not encompass the beauty . . . existence . . . life . . . God . . . love.

5. "Describe briefly a serious adverse personal situation and how you handled it."

   I have realized many times that I can neither do good or be good, do right or be right, by myself. The Prayer Book phrase is, "There is no health in us*"—by ourselves. It can be handled only by grace—a gift, that is, from God. We cannot generate it.

---

*This phrase, omitted from the 1979 version, was found in the General Confession in the 1928 version of the Book of Common Prayer, pp. 6, 23.

How are you doing? Two more.

6. "State your honest attitude toward alcoholic drinks."

My response to that is—enough is enough.

7. "How do you face a new day?"

In my experience, it depends.

Now here are some further questions that I am just going to identify because they will identify the college for you.

1. Have you ever put on clown make-up? When? For what purpose? When did you first "dress up?"

2. When did you first think of becoming a circus clown?

3. Why do you think you would make a funny clown?

4. Circle the circus skills in which you are adept: Acrobatics. Baton-twirling. Juggling. Pantomime. Stilt-walking. Unicycle riding. Wire-walking. Other." I can juggle three tennis balls with two hands.

Well, these questions are taken from the application blank for admission to Ringling Brothers & Barnum and Bailey Circus Clown College, P.O. Box 1528, Venice, Florida, in case you are interested. They are questions that ought to be attached to every college application blank. They reflect insights into learning for life by learning how to deal with all human experiences, not just intellectual ones or rational ones that are subject to reason and the intellect, but into that infinitely greater variety of experiences in life that are utterly irrational and are not subject to reason because they do not make any sense. The comic and the tragic, those elements of existence are the subject matter for the clown.

Pain . . . did you ever know any real pain that could be explained scientifically? Goodness . . . did you ever try to have an intellectual try to explain the mystery of goodness in life? The goodness of a mother is just as powerful a fact as "two plus two equals four." Who can explain it? Humor . . . absurdity . . . falling flat on your face . . . (especially when you are pompous) . . . accepting the incongruities of life . . . shoes too big so you walk funny . . . firecrackers exploding unexpectedly to trip you up . . . the slings of outrageous fortune throwing a pie in your face . . . you shrug your shoulders, wipe off your face, laugh and pick yourself up, and you go tripping along in life.

Someone has said that "life is what happens to you when you are making other decisions." That is the way life is. We have to make decisions and we have to use our judgment, but what life brings is what happens to us when we are making those decisions. To learn how to deal with these experiences of life is as important as learning the Second Law of Thermodynamics or how many divisions there were in ancient Gaul. It is an ironic satisfaction that knighthood is to be bestowed on Charles Chaplin and P. J. Wodehouse. They are knights. They are knights, of course, of faith. The experiences that are revealed in them and by clowns are experiences because they are the subject matter of life. They begin to make it possible for people to appropriate those experiences; and the curriculum of Clown College humanizes the curriculum of human existence. It brings both a tragic and a joyful dimension to what so often is an arid learning experience. Have you been on a college campus recently? There is not much fun, not much joy, not much delight in existence.

Well, the theme of this sermon is, I trust, clear. The clown represents the foolishness of faith. It is only faith, trust in the divine foolishness of God that makes life not only bearable but totally human, encompassing both the heights and the depths of life, giving it some sense of direction, ability to cope, movement and purpose, meaning. What to faithless eyes is an absolutely meaningless existence, to the eyes of faith may provide the ground of hope. Rather than despair because of the irrationality of life it may become the way toward renewed life. The depths and the surging power that comes out of the depths of existence when pain has descended (always unfairly) brings a dimension and an understanding of the mystery of the human enterprise that never comes when life is flat out on the surface. What is "death on the Cross" becomes an entrance into a hope and a vision. What is "pain" may be an offering to a new more profound way of life.

It really is kind of *funny* when you think of it, that when you realize that there is absolutely no hope in yourself to become the person you want to become that that is when there is the greatest hope that God will transform you into the person he wants you to become. It is really *absurd* that once you realize you are not in control of life you can begin to enjoy it and to trust it and to live. It is really *fantastic* that when you set goals in terms of what *you* want and you attain those goals, you discover you do not want them. If you set your heart on what God wants, then things begin to fall into place. Or if you just set your heart upon trying to find out what God wants, then things begin to fall into place and you can begin to rejoice, enjoy, and accept more and more things.

That last question, "How do you face a new day?" It is *ridiculous*. But here is an answer. It is ridiculous that

> creation crouches at the
> doorstep of every day
> watching for happening . . .
> And when event transfigures life,
> creation holds its breath—
> and cries out,
> Praise God.

Ridiculous, just plain ridiculous that creation crouches at the doorstep of your life every day. Watching for the event to transfigure life so that your life cries out, "Praise God." So, creation, God, life—all working through every human experience, through your fantasies and dreams, as well as through your failures, through your pains, and your joys, to transform, to transfigure, renew you every day.

The *fantastic* story of God loving the world so much that he sends his son to die so that life can begin day by day for you and for me. What a clown God must be! Very funny . . . Very scary . . . Very holy.

How do you face a new day? Creation is holding its breath for you to trust God so that the events of the day may transfigure your life so that you and all creation may cry out, Praise God! Amen.

The Truth
Plus the Person
Equals Life

———✺———

The Second Sunday after Epiphany,
January 19, 1975

H e who has the son has life; he who has not the son has not life."
True or false?

As you look at your life and as you look at the lives of others whom
you know, as well as one person can know another person, is it true that
those who have the son in fact *do* have life? And those who have not the
son do *not*? This is a true or false question. It follows the questions that
were asked last week—the application blank into the university of life.

The theme today is about ideas. It has to do with ways of possessing
ideas of the truth, of learning those ideas that claim to represent truth,
of possessing truth so that we have life and of passing that life and truth
on to others. Living is always in relationship to others, and this sermon
is meant to complement last week's sermon which was about persons.
We were concerned then, some of you will recall, about becoming whole
people. How do we recognize and acknowledge all of the aspects of our
life, our dream world and fantasy world as well as the demonic world
within us, the tragic and the comic of life as well as the rational? How
do we incorporate as many aspects of life as we can within ourselves and
balance them as well as we can, so that we may really live fully as people, so that as we mature—that is as we are educated by the experiences
of life—we mature not *only* intellectually? That intellectual maturity is
what schools and colleges too exclusively are concerned with—the edu-

cation of the mind—but in addition to that we must be concerned with our emotional maturity, our ability to incorporate the tragic and the funny things that happen, our intuitive response to the wholeness of experience, as well.

Well, today, if we can, we would like to try to put these two themes together—that is, ideas and persons—because what we all desire is to become true people, right people, whole people. And it might be said that we become in the long run the ideas we consider to be true. The ideas that we believe in and commit ourselves to in the long run determine who we become. If we believe, for example, that might makes right, we tend to become little fascists in our circle of acquaintances. The father who considers himself the absolute head of the household, because he is male and the breadwinner, tends to become an authoritarian tyrant. On the other hand, a person who has the idea that the ideal goal in life is never to get your own way but to accept everything that comes indiscriminately and never to stand for justice, to accept all the injustices of life because that is what he believes he deserves, tends to become a Caspar Milquetoast, a sentimentalist. He mollycoddles other people and himself. He becomes a mollycoddler. And those around him carry on their existence in response to a person who stands for nothing, no discrimination. I use these illustrations to point to the relationship between ideas and persons. The idea of truth that we hold, the truth that we put our confidence in, tends to determine the kinds of persons we become.

It is necessary, therefore, this morning to turn our attention to this question of truth. The statement is made, "In him you have life." Is that true or is that sentimental? This question of truth, how we discover it, relate to it, consciously and unconsciously, helps form us so we show forth what we believe to be true by what we become. Now this question, "What is truth?" is of course as old as mankind. It has been perhaps the theme more than any other theme that has created history.

Astrologers tried to find the answers in the stars. Parts of our subculture have not advanced beyond that. Put a dollar bill in the computer, and the stars, computerized now, will tell you the meaning of your life. Farmers in primitive societies tended to find the meaning in the flooding of their lands by the river; growth came; the fields became fertile; fertility cults think they possess truth. *Everything You Ever Wanted to Know about Sex, The Joy of Sex*, more and better sex, infinite varieties of sex—that is the truth for untold people in our culture who find meaning around ancient fertility or lack of fertility. Primitive tribes sometimes search for answers in the spirit world—the grove, the mountain, the river— open to the spirit, one was possessed by the spirits and therefore found meaning. Today people find meaning in the spirit of *absolute* peace of mind, of *absolute* unity with God, of absolute confidence that they possess the word of God. So sophisticated cultures try to find the answer to the search for truth rationally.

Let us reason together, so if you will pardon a gross historical distortion, it is possible to say that mankind founded centers through his experience which are still nourishing people in Western culture. It might be said that the search for truth finally centered in two towns—one in Athens, and the other in Jerusalem—and that the sources for our present understanding of the meaning of existence, whether it is the astrologers, or whether it is Freud, or whether it is psychiatry, or whether it is science, or whether it is religion, all reflect those early sources of searching. We continue to be replenished by the greatness of that search—that comes out of those two centers.

Athens was the home of Plato who through Socrates declared that "the gentle art of reason" was the best way to enter into the meaning of the world of ideas and so discover what is true. Jerusalem, on the other hand, was the native home for the people of faith, and they said they found God *revealed himself*, and you could not possibly search for him and find him by your own reason. His ways are not our ways; his ways are different ways. But if you will live in a community, and accept the fact of your existence in the tribe of Israel and will open yourself, he will speak to you. And he led them out of the wilderness and out of slavery and into a promised land whose capital city was Jerusalem. Faith is the way to truth. The Jewish people and the Christian people, both peoples of faith, found their spiritual home in Jerusalem. They searched out the mystery of God and found him, they said, by faith. That is what is truth.

This contribution of Athens—the life of reason, rational discourse, see what the facts are, examine them, Aristotle, Plato—that of course is the basis for the culture of the West more than any other, the basis for the scientific revolution. We find ourselves in nature, and nature is given us so that we can harness her, control her, exploit her—she is there for our purposes. The results are perfectly obvious in our contemporary technological society. The contribution of Jerusalem, on the other hand, has been the declaration that behind nature is God who is the God of all of creation, and the only way to use nature is by serving God. The way to truth is not to try to control God or try to exploit him or to use him—

that is *magic*–but to acknowledge him, worship him, try to serve him. And service of him is expressed in serving mankind.

So these two worlds–roughly and again in a very distorted fashion, the scientific and the religious worlds, the world of reason and the world of faith–continue to be the two ways in our culture by which mankind comes to perceive what is true, and which inform persons today how to become true persons. You can identify, and again too sharply, the person who is coldly analytical, whose life is planned out, and the person who senses he is related to a power or a spirit beyond his control. Most of us go back and forth between those two ways as we mature. Certain things we think we can control; other things over which we have no control obviously impinge upon us and sometimes will direct and even destroy us. We use sometimes the word "humanist" or "theist"–not very accurately–to suggest the one person who says, "Life is what you see" and the other person who says, "There is more to life than meets the eye."

I have taken the time to give this oversimplified distortion of history because it is sometimes helpful to recognize that the options (which seem to us to be terribly contemporary and to have just flown into our society and culture) have been in fact as old as history, and that we are simply now taking our place in the exploration of the fascinating mystery of what is true about existence. Furthermore, if we can put Athens and Jerusalem in a perspective–reason and faith–we can see that these two worlds are *both* ways toward truth. It is a false antithesis that is set up which says that if you are a man of reason, you cannot be a man of religion; or if you are a man of religion, you have to be a man of blind faith. They are not the same. Sometimes they overlap; sometimes they are in conflict; but truth–that is, God–is so extraordinary in the dimensions of his existence that he encompasses all of creation.

The modern counterparts of Athens and Jerusalem might be the university and the church. The one is the custodian of learning, sometimes in a very narrow sense; the other is the custodian of faith, also sometimes in a very narrow sense. But both nurture the human enterprise, and both promise ways for persons to mature as whole persons. You become most whole as persons of the twentieth century by belonging both to the world of learning and to the world of faith. And again, that is too sharp because it is increasingly obvious to men of science that science is built upon faith, and discoveries of science are results of affirmations of faith that people have been willing to risk. And faith, if it is to be a true faith that will encompass all the facts of life including those comic and tragic elements that we discussed last week, must be a rational one as well.

Now you may ask, "What on earth is he carrying on like this for, giving what seems to be a lecture, rather than a sermon?" Well, I will tell you. (Thank you for asking.)

We are coming, in my judgment, into a period in our society—that is the society of the Western world—when these two worlds, reason and faith, learning and religion, the university and the church, are obviously moving closer together. And together they hold some promise that we may be led out of the impasse to which we have come. Technological society alone with its perfection of the means of production and marketing, its control and exploitation of nature, has obviously been primarily responsible for bringing us into our present state. That domination of technology seems to have run its course, at least in the sense that the experts of the scientific view of life are incapable today of moving this society forward with any kind of respect for the personhood of persons, with respect for the humanity of human beings. Witness famine, wars, unemployment—all subject to reason—but reasonable man cannot deal with them by reason alone. The humility which follows from this recognition—how the mighty are fallen—the humility which follows from this kind of recognition is the one indispensible condition necessary for the recognition of our common brotherhood as members of the human race under a common God. And for those who do not have that kind of faith, the recognition of a common brotherhood—that we are all bound together—the perception of that relationship, and the striving for justice which follows from it in society, is what the world of religion at its best is all about. To be sure, the church gets obsessed by its own inner life sometimes (*most* of the time), but it always points just beyond to that God, and allegiance to God and to reason together promise the most for wholeness.

So the reason for this sermon is to set before you, as we enter into a new chapter in our nation's history with a new President and a new Congress, a renewed hope that as we take time in this congregation to become intelligent men and women of faith, that we may make our contribution toward the renewal of our country as we become renewed as Christian people.

Athens and Jerusalem—centers of ideas—are in the final analysis held together always by people. And Christian people point to those two worlds held together in their community of faith as promising the most in serving mankind—not because they are so great—but because they are gathered together and centered around the person Jesus Christ, full of grace and truth. That is, he who holds the two worlds of reason and faith together.

As the church is faithful, it offers a community of faith. It welcomes and accepts people—all kinds of people—just as they are, and it promises to serve them—to serve mankind—because that is what the truth of God is, seen in him who accepts and forgives us that we may serve others. Do you want life and to live? Do you want to make as great a contribution as you can to your society and to your family and your nation? "He who has the son has life; he who does not have the son has not life." True or False?

> O Lord Jesus Christ,
> When we are in touch with the truth about ourselves,
>   we are in touch with you.
> So we thank you for showing us some truth about
>   ourselves, and so about you.
> We turn to you because you call us,
>   and have already come to us.
> As we respond to the truths we know,
>   we shall come at last to know you
>   who art the truth full of grace.
> In the meantime, help us to live and love you,
>   our neighbors, our nation, and ourselves.
> Amen.

In Time Like Glass

—ᴍ—

The Last Sunday after Epiphany,
February 9, 1975

One of the journeys I have always dreamed of taking (and probably never will) is to go from Damascus across the desert to Teheran and Isfahan, then to Kabul in Afghanistan, from there to Sinkiang in Central Asia, and then to go down to Nepal and Katmandu, finally to India. As a matter of fact, I used to dream about this trip and even invited our youngest daughter to accompany me on it when she graduated from college. But she grew up and got married and so has another better companion, even though neither one of us may ever get to Sinkiang.

I can almost say, "Never mind," because I have recently completed the same trip in the company of the author of a book, Evelyn Ames, who has described almost precisely that dream trip of mine (except for Sinkiang) in a book entitled *In Time Like Glass*. It is a superb travel book, not only because of the outward journey that is described, but because it is also a description of an inward journey. The outer and the inner go hand-in-hand. She is able through the outward, physical description of the people and places to describe the inner scene of the spirit that is revealed through them.

As all true artists of the inner landscape, she illumines our own inner journey, so that by reading of her trip we can see more clearly what is going on in the inward journey that we all take. (So in addition to those Lenten books that are recommended in the leaflet, let me add *In Time Like Glass* by Evelyn Ames.)

Well, having now returned from this journey with her, let me try to describe just one aspect of what she has helped me to see in my own inner journey. Let me ask you whether it corresponds in any measure with anything that you have discovered yourself in your own experience, and then conclude with a specific description that she gives of one place which seems to me to sum up the meaning of our common journey in the mystery of our common existence.

The single aspect of human experience that I want to describe—or perhaps, more accurately, *identify*—is its split, its division, the polarities, tensions, sometimes its tearing. The wholeness of life seems to be able to be described only by identifying opposites—darkness and light, male and female, confidence and timidity, trust and fear, creation and destruction, love and hate, compassion and selfishness, togetherness and loneliness, alienation and reconciliation, depression and euphoria, desolation and joy, pain and peace, yes and no. You can, from your own experience, add almost any number of divisions, oppositions, polarities like these.

One of the discoveries that I make as I take my own inward journey is that the division is *within* me. I am divided. I am not the person I want to be. I am not even the person I claim to be. I have at times high resolves and meager accomplishments. The road to hell, we say, is paved with good intentions. That road gets new paving blocks from me every day. Think of how many New Year's Resolutions are now, one month later, strewn all over the roads of peoples' journeys.

The division is deeper, however, than just not keeping promises or resolutions. In fact there seems to be on a deeper level something that is at work within me that is set deliberately against my doing what I want to do, or ought to do, or hope to do. I want to do good, but I do not do it. Why not? I would like to be good, but I am not. Why is that? And sometimes, the very hurt that I want to avoid giving is *exactly* what I do give to people. It is as if there were some power, some demon that possesses me and prevents me from being the whole person that I want to be.

Do you ever have this experience? When you are quiet and look within and describe your own inner pilgrimage, do you observe that no matter how hard you try to overcome this kind of division, you do not overcome it, except once in a while? There is something that seems to be working within you to prevent it. And so you live in fact a divided, double kind of life, one kind of motion within you which is impelling you toward wholeness and another which is preventing it.

Now just one other observation of this description: As I look around, and try to understand the division in my own nature, I see that *outside* nature itself apparently is divided. There is both feast and famine. There are rains that come to nourish the crops, and the rains turn into typhoons that uproot the crops. The stars move in their ordered courses, while earthquakes rumble and shake the foundations of the earth; the earth opens up and swallows cities and people. They are consumed. Destruction seems to be as much a part of nature as creation. Nature itself is divided.

The only guarantee that nature promises when she gives birth to life is that life will die. (We live, interestingly enough, creatively, as we are able more and more to move into the acceptance of our never living— the acceptance of dying.) Life and death is that ultimate division which is the mark of our journey as human beings. That outward journey is the reflection of our inner journey, or perhaps it is the other way around—our inner journey reflected in the outer journey. But in either case, or both, one aspect of our journey is our split, its division, its tearing, the polarities—the creative and the destructive.

One further observation and then the quotation from the book. The observation is this: the polarities, the tensions between the polarities, are *unbearable*. We just cannot honor both sides of our nature wholly. We cannot be both wholly creative and wholly destructive. We cannot say both "yes" and "no." We cannot both love with all our strength and hate with all our strength without breaking. And if we do not do something, that is of course just what happens—we break. We have what we call "breakdowns." We fly apart, or we try to have one part of our nature control, destroy, repress another side; and whatever the destruction and repression is, the response to it always emerges flying, breaking, fragmenting.

So we tend, therefore, most of us, to back away from this tension, because it is too tight and too unbearable—to back away from living as fully as we can in accordance with our nature. We temper ourselves. We moderate our desires. We try to control our natures, and so we develop what we call "character traits." Character traits always limit, cut off, in some way the fullness of our dual nature. We try to put reins on our passions—passions for goodness or passions for evil. We know, for example, that if we do not love very much, we are not going to get hurt very much. If we do not really hate anybody, we probably are going to escape their notice, and we will not get hate in return. We tend at the extreme to not only moderate our passions, but finally to give up all passion for anything—good or bad—to settle for just as little as we can. So if we are not involved, we will not suffer pain. This giving-up process ultimately, of course, is a giving up of life. It is a slow death, a slow death of the spirit, though the flesh may endure. Probably nothing is worse than to be dead and still be walking, to have the spirit collapse so that there is no life, no zip, no nothing except enduring.

Well, the other way to deal with this tension or these polarities is to deliberately take them and to transfer them, to take them and to give them to a power outside ourselves—be it a good power or a bad power—something that transcends, controls, is more important than we are. It is to say, "Here is my nature, this divided nature. You integrate it! Integrate it around hate or love, greed or justice, whatever—something other than our nature—more powerful than our divided nature." It is to declare for Christian people that there is another power that is more powerful than the demonic power within us that divides us—that seems to possess us. And in the Christian story, that seems to be splitting us all the time or trying to split us.

If we can give ourselves with all our nature into that power, then the possibility of transcending our nature, of integrating our nature, of transforming our nature then becomes part and parcel of the motion in life. People who do this do not have to therefore deny their natures or pretend that they are something they are not. It is to affirm them and put them in the hands or in the service of one whom they trust. That is Christian living. However poorly it may be done, it is always a transfer of our nature into the hands of another power more powerful than we are. It is that which makes possible the creative tension or dynamic living within ourselves with all our being, so that we can love most fully, most passionately, be driven for good and for justice, so all divisions are held together and given over to that transcendent power. For Christian people, the name is *Christ*. But it is the same power in non-Christian cultures. It is a power that is at work always for wholeness, holding good and evil and transforming the passions, the life, the nature of men and women, so that they may live fully and freely and help others live.

Well, let me summarize this with a quotation now of a description from this book. Toward the end of the journey, the travelers came to Bombay and there they set out one day in a small boat in the harbor for the island of Elephanta where there is a series of cave temples. It is an hour away. They landed and climbed up to the top of the hill to one of the great holy places of India. The temples there within the caves, or within the overhanging of the rocks, are dedicated to Shiva, the god who possesses all of the characteristics of existence—creative, disruptive, male, female—the supreme deity who has merging within him the characteristics of Brahma and Vishnu, the creator and the preserver, the great goddess.

The central cave at the top of this hill is fifty yards deep and fifty yards wide. There are stone carvings at the entrance and around the sides—bas reliefs—in which the dual nature of Shiva is depicted, different contradictory aspects—one where the god is dancing and the other where the god is meditating—the same god—the god of motion and the god of stillness; the god who is male and the god who is female; the god who is violent and the god who is gentle. Well, the culmination of these is the central image against the inner wall opposite the opening. Here is Mrs. Ames' description:

> Our group, silent and attentive, was now drawn toward the central image against the inner wall facing the entrance, and known as the Mahesamurti: the twenty-foot-tall triple head of the Supreme Shiva, fully manifest. To the left, seen in profile and in deep shadow, is the face of violent aggression and destruction, with a serpent held in one raised hand; to the right and also in profile, the powerfully creative and protective face of the feminine principle, the hand holding a lotus. Centered between them, eyes closed, is the sublime transcendence of these and of all opposites which tear the individual being apart or combine in creative tension—a head which is the image of elate calm, of majesty, and of containment totally free of time and space.
>
> I looked and saw what I didn't know existed: divinity made visible—and in human guise. I was stunned and struck with recognition—both: here was something which had always been missing yet I hadn't known that it was. Faces transfigured by emotion may hint at it but are only approximations; those in paintings and sculptures of saints and angels and heroes; of Christ and his apostles—of whatever period or region—feel like sketches for it but however perfect in themselves, however great as art, they have not yet arrived at this ultimate spiritual grandeur.
>
> What are the closed eyes contemplating? What being is so at peace with the turmoil, horror, and delights of the world? Though human, the face is that of the Bhagavad-Gita's 'This (which) never is born and never dies, nor may it after being come again to be not; this unborn, everlasting, abiding Ancient . . . not slain when the body is slain . . .'
>
> What was immediately clear . . . was that a particular 'idol,' or at least this one, can be a beacon and touchstone, visible evidence of things unseen as a tree is of the wind. Not till months later did I see that what had 'come over me' and, apparently, over all of us in the dim cave was

the inherence of spirit in matter, the presence of the unchanging and absolute in what is temporal and ephemeral. What else is that but 'the kingdom of heaven within you'? In the Mahesamurti, God's presence, God immanent in Man, is made manifest. In a cave temple in India, the message of Christ is realized.

. . . The face is human and it is also divine; the face is in stone . . . yet the stone is also spirit. Seeing substance and spirit so inseparably one, the familiar sense of being split into two dissolves away . . .

The reality is that man and God are one; and that our true nature is made whole in Christ, who is both God and man.

Mrs. Ames dedicates her book to all "the guides and companions" she has known on her own inner journey. We dedicate whatever we write in describing the journey of our lives to those guides and companions who are the bearers of Christ. So we dedicate in this service a room—physical wood—where the spirit of Bromwell Ault and the spirit of all those who have lifted us in the communion of the spirit—fellow travelers, music, God, man, substance—dwell, wholly one in Christ.

Let us now in the name of God dedicate to his glory and for the service of this church the Bromwell Ault Music Room.

O God, before whose throne the saints and the goodly fellowship of all those who have departed this life in your faith and fear and who now rejoice in their full life in you, bless we pray you this music room which we dedicate to the memory of Bromwell Ault with thanksgiving for his life, what he did, how he did it, for himself, and for the spirit of grace which he bore. Grant that the voices that sing here may sing of your glory and may call the members of this congregation to worship you. May we continually lift our hearts unto you with all who dwell in the company of saints forever and ever. Amen.

Ash Wednesday Homily
On Lincoln's Birthday

—⟋⟍—

Ash Wednesday, February 12, 1975

Penitence—repentance—sins—confession—
discipline—fasting—prayer—self-denial.

Those are all Ash Wednesday words. They remind us of the words that are on the other side of Easter: *forgiveness—hope—new life—faith—resurrection—love—a new creation.*

It would be dishonest, unrealistic of us if, on Ash Wednesday, we did not pause to identify those sins, recognize them, confess them, offer them, determine to the best of our ability that we will no longer be bound by them, try to lead ordered lives, and so begin to show forth in some measure the Easter spirit of hope and forgiveness and joy and new life. Easter and Ash Wednesday in God's time are the same time. That is now.

So we begin Lent as individuals with our confession of personal sins and our personal hopes to be fulfilled in the Easter story. But we do so also as American people, citizens of this country. So Ash Wednesday, particularly on this day, is also a day for our recognition of our national sins and our national hopes. It is this dimension which is brought forth with particular poignancy on the birthday of Abraham Lincoln, the one who called the American people "the almost chosen people."* Perhaps

---

*Speech to the New Jersey State Senate, February 21, 1862. See http://showcase .netins.net/web/creative/lincoln/speeches/quotes.htm.

more than any other President, save Washington, he had that deep sense of the Providence of God directing the destiny of this nation, and in his own decisions he always appealed beyond human decisions in the direction of the God who directs history. "Our political problem now," he wrote, "is, can we, as a nation, continue together permanently—forever—half slave and half free? The problem is too mighty for me. May God, in his mercy, superintend the solution."*

We as a nation continue not fully free, not fully just. The political problem is beyond us. May God in his mercy superintend the solution. It was that turning of himself and of his nation to God's superintendence that marked Lincoln's political decisions. It was that kind of reliance upon God that enabled him on one occasion to respond to a clergyman who had said he hoped "the Lord was on our side" by saying, "I'm not at all concerned about that, for I know that the Lord is *always* on the side of the *right*. And it is my constant anxiety and prayer that I and *this nation* shall be on the Lord's side."**

So this Lent, as we examine our personal short-comings and live by hope in the new life in Christ, we are asked also to examine our nation's short-comings, our nation's falling short of that land of liberty and equality and justice that has been placed before us which we have been "called" to establish. We repent in the face of God's judgment in order that we may be given hope, a renewed life, and a deepened sense of destiny under God as his "almost chosen people" so that we can go ahead with a renewed sense of God's direction.

So as we move through Lent, and this year into next year, a new chapter in our nation's history, may it be with the spirit of that great, tragic, noble, good, patient, honest leader who wanted himself and his nation to be under the direction of God and on the Lord's side, who was able in his second Inaugural Address to conclude: "with malice toward none; with charity for all; with firmness in the right, as God gives us to see the right, let us strive on to finish the work we are in; to bind up the nation's wounds; to care for him who shall have borne the battle, and

---

*Letter to Judge George Robertson, August 15, 1855. See http://myloc.gov/Exhibitions/lincoln.

**See http://quotationsbook.com/quote/45422/.

for his widow, and his orphan—to do all which may achieve and cherish a just and a lasting peace among ourselves and with all nations."

This Ash Wednesday is an appropriate day for us to look ahead to a new day for our nation, of justice and of peace, among ourselves and with all nations. And this we shall try to do on the Sundays in Lent. Amen.

Let Us Choose Life —
A Sermon for Our Country

—ɯɯ—

The First Sunday in Lent,
February 16, 1975

"Thou art the man." The accusation of Nathan the Prophet against David the King is simple, direct, and devastating. "You are the one who is guilty."

David is found out. He has taken the wife of one of his captains, gone to bed with her, arranged to have her husband killed, married her. When he is accused by Nathan the Prophet, the only reply he can make is, "I have sinned against the Lord."

Have you ever been found out? Have you ever had anyone say to you, "You're the one. You are the unfaithful person; you are the disloyal one; you are the unjust one. Look at what has been given you, the heritage that is yours. Look at what you have done with that heritage. You are the man. You are the woman."

Well, if you have ever had the experience of being found out, or if you have even had the sense of what if somebody *did* find out—you know there is not much you can do except say, "You are right. That is just the way I am. I have sinned." And if you have any religious conviction at all, you can add, "I have sinned against the Lord."

To identify with David, you don't have to have committed adultery nor put anybody to death. There is in the fabric of life itself a judgment that is laid upon us, not so much, perhaps, because of incidents, as that is just the way we are. We know we deserve to be judged. That is our nature—the disposition that we have. And when we are accused, we can say, "You are right. That is the kind of person I am." So in our most honest moments, when we don't have to protect ourselves anymore and we are willing to be absolutely vulnerable, we confess our nature, our sin. Usually it is very personal, very subjective, very private, deeply emotional. You can search your memories this morning or your hearts to identify those actions or that disposition in your heart that would prompt you, when you hear an accusation, "Thou art the one," to reply, "That's right. I have sinned. I have sinned against the Lord."

Let me now ask you to take this sense of judgment that is somehow built into life and the sense that judgment always is just. (And if a particular accusation is unfair, then there are other accusations that might be made that would be devastatingly fair). Let me ask you to take this sense of judgment which we experience as individuals and see how it is also part and parcel of our corporate life and, in particular, our national life. We are not simply persons, period. We are American persons, in a particular nation at a particular time with a particular heritage, with a particular climate. And whoever we are, we cannot describe ourselves simply in personal terms. We belong to a people. The meaning of our existence, as individuals, is inextricably bound up with the meaning of our nation.

Tomorrow is celebrated as Washington's birthday, and today is the first Sunday in Lent. It seems providential. Next year we are moving into an anniversary celebration of two-hundred years, and if we are going to celebrate who we are as a nation, we have to be prepared in a more meaningful way than we are prepared in our nation to date. My personal guess is we will be and that there will be an extraordinary thrust forward in our nation by the time we come to the end of 1976.

How do we get prepared to become renewed? How do we recapture that sense of destiny under God that he has, in fact, brought forth on this continent a new people—to create a new world to serve the nations of the world? How can there be rekindled that light which promises in the beacon held high "liberty and justice for all"? How can we see more clearly with bright eyes that vision that, "We shall be a City set on a Hill" with the eyes of all peoples upon us?

That phrase, "We shall be as a City upon a Hill," comes from a sermon that was preached by the first leader of the Massachusetts Bay Colony, John Winthrop, in 1630. He was on a ship approaching these shores. In that sermon, he set forth the spirit that prompted those early settlers to come to this land and which has caused us in our day to declare, by vote of Congress, that we are in fact a nation "under God."

"Thus stands the course between God and us," he preached. "We are entered into Covenant with him for this work; we have taken out a Commission; the Lord hath given us leave to draw our own articles; we have professed to enterprise these actions upon these and these ends; we have besought him of favor and blessing. Now if the Lord shall please to hear us, and bring us in peace to the place we desire, then hath he ratified this Covenant and sealed our Commission. . . . We must consider that we shall be as a City upon a Hill, the eyes of all people are upon us . . .

"Therefore," he concludes, "Let us choose life, that we, and our seed, may live; by obeying his voice, and cleaving to him, for he is our life, and our prosperity."

There was a covenant, a contract, an agreement by faith between God and the people whom he chose. It is a biblical reading of history. God is involved in the history of the peoples who chose him and whom he chooses. He chose the people of Israel, called them out of slavery in Egypt, delivered them through the terrors of the Red Sea, brought them to safety before the mountain of Sinai where he gave the Ten Commandments as the symbol of that Covenant; and then led them through the wilderness to the Promised Land. So now, within this perspective of understanding our history, he entered into a Covenant with Christian people leading them out of oppression in England, calling them across the sea to a new land, a Promised Land where there should be freedom and justice for all. The Covenant was signed and sealed in that company as they pledged allegiance to one another and to God—the Mayflower Compact—and then later, by all the peoples of this nation, as they signed in their hearts the Declaration of Independence in 1776. It is an extraordinary story of people giving birth to a new nation as they obeyed the One who had given them, they believed, this land—to be a City upon a Hill for the eyes of all peoples to look upon.

In the Prayer Book there is a *Prayer For Our Country.** It was put there in 1928. It was written in the last century at the suggestion of William Reed Huntington, then rector of Grace Church in New York, by the clergyman who was rector of the Episcopal Church in Bristol, Rhode Island, the Reverend Lyman Locke. He was rector for fifty-one years. (They made them stronger in those days.) The prayer that he wrote first

---

*The prayer is found on p. 36 of the 1928 Book of Common Prayer and p. 820 of the 1979 version.

appeared in a prayer book called *The Book Annexed,* 1883. He begins it with the theme that was set forth by Winthrop: "Almighty God, who in former time didst lead our fathers forth into a wide and beautiful land. . . ." That phrase was changed by 1928 to read, "Almighty God, who hast given us this good land for our heritage. . . ." During the Sundays in Lent we shall try to draw out some of the implications of this prayer that follow for our day, particularly as we look ahead.

Today there are just two implications that conclude this sermon. They are both related to David's adultery—and to your own adulteries of spirit, if not of body—your own sense of conviction of sin and the rightness of that judgment—and mine. The first is this: As David the man and David the king were the same person, so our personal life and our public, national life are inextricably bound together. The kind of nation we are reflects the kind of people we are. We get the leaders we deserve and want. If there are flaws in our national life, they reflect flaws in our personal lives. The accusation, "Thou art the man," goes directly to every citizen, and the first step to any kind of renewal in our land is to say, "I have sinned—I am responsible; I take my share of responsibility for the condition of this nation." With those of our fellow citizens who have a religious perspective upon life, we are able to say, "With them we have sinned against the Lord."

The other and final implication is very simply: If God has given us this land for our heritage, all we need do is treat it as such—a gift that comes from him for his people, for his purpose, to set a City on a Hill for the world—for all peoples. So we treat the land as his for all people— not to exploit it or its resources for a few people. And we treat all the people as his people—brothers and sisters, not the powerless exploited by the powerful. We do not exploit one another for the benefit of a few— the elite.

The prophet Nathan comes into our midst today and he asks, "What have you done with the land that was given you? You say you love your land—have you cared for it as though you loved it?" What can we say but "We have sinned against the Lord." The prophet Nathan comes to us today and he asks, "You who came seeking refuge from oppression as God's people, what did you do with the Indian people you found here on this land?" What can we say, as Americans except, "We have sinned, and sinned, and sinned beyond description with those people?" When he asks, "You who proclaim liberty and justice for all people, what did you do with the black people you bought and brought here?" What can we say except, "We have sinned, and sinned against the Lord?"

That cry of confession is a cry of hope, and there is no hope for this land if there is no cry of confession. It is a wonderful cry that promises untold new life for this nation. Just as it did for David. He became a great king—the kingdom of David's was the Kingdom of Israel. He renewed his people after he confessed, "I have sinned against the Lord."

God calls us to renewal by calling us to confession. He calls us to infinite hope by calling us to utter honesty. He calls us to new greatness by confessing our littleness. A new vision is there before us and a new life of a "City set on a Hill."

Therefore, let us choose life by obeying his voice and cleaving to him for he is our life and our prosperity.

Almighty God, you have given us this good land for our heritage; let us honor it for only so can we honor you. May we not be so anxious about how to use the land, as how the land might use us, by caring for it, conserving it, treating it gently with love. And since the people who dwell on the land are yours, forgive us for the way we have treated some as though they were ours.

Forgive us our sins against one another. Help us to redress ancient wrongs and to abolish present prejudices. Keep us faithful to you so we may perceive you in the fruit of the field as in the hearts and bodies of men—and so give unfeigned thanks to you by preserving your bounty and extending your justice among all your people, for all peoples. Since in you alone we live and move and have our being, let us choose life. Amen.

Celebration and Commitment—
Prayer for Our Country

—⁓—

The Fifth Sunday in Lent,
March 16, 1975

In an interview recorded in *The Washington Star* last month, John Warner, who is the head of the American Revolution Bicentennial Administration, was asked a series of questions about the Bicentennial—its problems, its programs, and opportunities.

The interview concluded with this question:

What would you like to see emerge from the Bicentennial?
First, a restoration in the people of their faith in themselves to achieve things, in other words, the community doing something for the Bicentennial rather than sitting back and letting the federal government do it all. I find as I cross the country a great despair that the individual cannot influence his daily life or even the eventual state of his family, and that's a discouraging thing. I believe the Bicentennial gives him an opportunity to get in and participate and do something and emerge saying to himself, "By golly, I count after all." The second, restore faith in the blueprint of our Nation—the Declaration of Independence, the Constitution, the Bill of Rights. I hope emerging from the Bicentennial will be a unanimous conviction of all Americans that those three great documents, that blueprint, was indeed laid down right and can carry us into the Third Century.

Mr. Warner could hardly have better described two of the three themes of this Lenten series on the *Prayer for Our Country*.* The first is,

---

*The prayer is found on p. 36 of the 1928 Book of Common Prayer and p. 820 of the 1979 version.

"By golly, I count after all." I am not just a private person. I am also a public citizen, and what I *do* as a person, who I *am* as a person has an effect on what our nation does and what our nation becomes. I belong to this country, and the life I lead privately influences, for good or ill, the public life of this nation. Our country is made up of persons who come to themselves most wholly always in relationship to other persons; and that begins in the family. That quality of life, of acceptance and love and sacrifice and hope begins in that early network of relationships of persons; it grows into wider and wider spheres beyond the personal family to all relationships in the community, in the city, in the family of this nation; and finally the family of this nation within the family of all nations. The quality of life in the world is determined in the first instance by the quality of life of the people.

Hence this theme of inter-relationships: "By golly, I count for something!" There is the second theme, the theme of loyalty to the best in our tradition—the Declaration of Independence, the Constitution, the Bill of Rights. "I hope emerging from the Bicentennial will be a unanimous conviction of all Americans that those three great documents, that blueprint, was indeed laid down right and can carry us into the Third Century."

As we have noted in this series not everything in our history is consistent with that blueprint—our treatment of the American Indian, the institution of slavery, the oppression of women and minority groups, our worship of success in materialistic terms, the worth of a person evaluated by the dollars he or she possesses, our exploitation of the land and her resources for individual rather than for the common good—to name but some of the flaws in our national character and heritage. But having said all of that, indeed saying it with honesty and with regret, it can also be said that the "noble experiment" has matured over two hundred years into a "noble experience." At our best, this country *has* been a light set on the hill for all peoples. It *has been* and continues to be down to today a place of refuge for people who have to flee from oppression and slavery and degradation and death, where there is *no* hope. Most of us in this church can remember how millions of Jews were burned to death simply because they were Jews. "The land of the brave and the home of the free" is an accurate description of our country in its nobility: all men *are* created equal. That's noble!

So we join with Mr. Warner in expressing the hope that the Bicentennial will bring about in the people a restoration of faith in themselves—

"By golly, I count after all!"—and what he calls the blueprint of our nation—the Declaration of Independence, the Constitution, and the Bill of Rights.

He identifies two of the three themes of this Lenten series, but not the third. He does not identify, nor perhaps should he, the architect who drew the blueprint. That is God. The blueprint is written into existence to apply over the face of the earth to all mankind. That blueprint was drawn before the creation of the world. It has been there since before the beginning, and it has been seen over the generations by those men and women who have had the eyes of faith to discern it. That is what the story of the Bible is about: men and women of faith seeing God in human history acting.

At the very dawn of history, according to a story first told by the Babylonians, and then retold by the Israelites, there was a flood that covered the earth. (It probably was a flood that covered only the Euphrates Valley, but that was the earth for those early inhabitants.) As the flood subsided, a rainbow appeared. Do you remember the excitement as a child when your parents pointed out the first rainbow—one end in the distance, one end in the clouds? The rainbow signifies God's promise never to forsake mankind. "This is the token, the sign of the covenant which I make between me and you and every living creature for all future generations." The rainbow appearing in the clouds is the sign, the promise of hope, of infinite hope. God never lets go—that is the reason that while there is life, there is always hope. Our hope is in the God of hope. So when we look forward to the Third Century, we can look forward with infinite hope because "In God is our trust"—the architect who gave us the blueprint to build a nation "with liberty and justice for all."

For Christians then, or perhaps more accurately for those who have the eyes of faith, God's hand is seen in human affairs. The greater the justice in any society, the greater the evidence of God's hand, for he is the one who created all men equal; and the laws of society are there to see that all men are treated that way. For those with that kind of an eye of faith, the Bicentennial provides us with an opportunity to see *him*, to have hope in *his* promise, to be encouraged more and more to respond to *him* by working for a more just family in our nation; in the words of the Prayer, "for peace and justice at home," a land with *more* equal opportunity. It is a time of hope; it *can* be a time of hope, as it is a time of dedication. Our *celebration*, the genuineness of it, will be reflected in our *commitment* to that blueprint. For Christian people, that is a commitment to God in Christ. So let us simply conclude by looking at Mr. Warner's two themes in the light of the third, in the light of the rainbow: God the architect.

First, "By golly, I count after all" becomes for the Christian who lives by hope, "By *God*, I count after all." What I do counts for God as well as for myself and for my country. And the central reason that I do anything is because I do it in response to *him*. When what I do, I try to do for him, then the meaning of my life begins to take on an eternal meaning and the meaning of my life does not depend then on what I do, or how successful I am, or how much money I make, or what I am able to accomplish. The promise of meaning is always in that which is greater than success. The leverage, the power for living, then comes from God. So I do not ever have to give up; I do not ever have to despair. When I count for something to God, then "By golly, I count for something." Faith in ourselves, faith in ourselves as persons, because our faith is in God—that is the first theme seen in the light of the rainbow.

The second, faith in the best of our tradition—the blueprint of human rights—because our faith is in God, the architect who created all men equal and who promises never to let us go. Therefore our nation counts after all. Our *nation* counts to God as well as to other nations. What we do in establishing greater justice for all sorts and conditions of men will determine what becomes of us as a nation.

God set his rainbow in the clouds as a symbol of his faithfulness to all mankind. We as part of that family of mankind serve him best when we are most faithful to the blueprint of justice and freedom he has already given us. When our nation has been great, it has been in obedience to *his* laws, when there has been peace and justice in our nation.

So the rainbow is the eternal sign of hope for all mankind that "the hand that made us is divine!" Amen.

Clap Your Hands,
All Ye People

—✽—

Palm Sunday, March 23, 1975

The sermon this Palm Sunday takes up where last year's sermon left off. Now in case that sermon does not come readily back to your mind, let me refresh your memory. It was entitled *On the Wisdom of Waving Palm Branches*. The waving of palm branches was an Oriental way of applauding, expressing respect, showing enthusiasm, honoring. "Hosanna! Blessed is he who comes in the name of the Lord, even the King of Israel." So on Palm Sunday, we applaud Jesus as he rides into Jerusalem. We applaud him as he rides into our lives. We stand in the crowd as the procession goes by; we wave our palm branches. He is on his way. Our story is going to be unfolded once again. The sermon ended with a reminder that in the Orient it is often the custom when a speaker or a performer is applauded that he applauds back to the audience. So these concluding words: "Can you see Jesus going by on the donkey's back? He has a palm branch. He is waving at you. Wave back. Wave together, to the glory of God the Father. Amen."

You have had moments like that, haven't you, when everything seemed just right? Everything fell into place, and you could hardly keep from bursting because you were so filled with the exuberance of life, the glory of just being alive. So you burst into song, or you skipped along the path, or you clapped your hands and cried, "O God, O God, O God!" Great! And as you waved your palm branch, applauding God, you had the sense somehow that he was waving back at you. That is, he was rejoicing in your existence just as much as you were. Everything fits together.

If you have ever had such a personal experience, you know that it does not depend upon your being a perfect person. You can still have plenty of faults and failures. You can be quite *imperfect* in fact. And the event does not depend upon your own morality. It depends rather on your being put in touch with existence, being put in tune with existence. It is a "happening" which simply happens—puts you in touch with a reality which unifies you, possesses you, that lifts you up, that inspires you, transforms you. And you cannot do anything at such moments except applaud. "O God!" You clap your hands and you cry, "God!" You celebrate.

From "On the Wisdom of Waving Palm Branches" last year, we have this year "Clap Your Hands, All Ye People!" It is about the celebration for our nation. It is one of the series this Lent about our life in this country centered around the *Prayer for Our Country,** looking forward to the Bicentennial next year. It has to do with how we can best prepare ourselves for a national "happening," so that we may celebrate as a nation whose people have come together—where everything or almost everything falls into place, where there is a common sense of purpose and direction and enthusiasm, excitement—some sense of exultation because we belong to this country—some sense of being inspired, filled with the spirit of this nation at its best, so we are proud to belong. We search not so much for ways to celebrate but for a reason to celebrate. How can we make it possible for a "happening" to happen, so we cannot as a nation help ourselves but to celebrate, to clap our hands, all people? How can we wave our palm branches as citizens?

The prayer that was read this morning, the *Prayer for Our Country,* puts it very directly: ". . . that through obedience to thy law we may show forth thy praise among the nations of the earth." As simple as that. God's law is the law of justice, which judges every law of mankind and gives a direction to every law of mankind, so that the more the laws of men correspond to the law of God, the greater the celebration for God. It is the law of justice, because God is a just God. It is the law of fairness, because God is a fair God. He does not play any favorites. All people are his. He does not see any difference between a baby who is born in the New York Hospital and a baby who is born in a cold water flat in Harlem. He loves both equally, and he wants them to be treated fairly,

*The prayer is found on p. 36 of the 1928 Book of Common Prayer and p. 820 of the 1979 version.

with justice and liberty for both. The nation that is concerned to make that kind of justice increasingly possible always has something to celebrate, because there is always a dynamic and a moving and a purpose. There is always a spirit. And if the citizens of any land or our land do not *care,* just do not *care* what happens to one another, then there will not be any celebration because there will not be any people coming together. It is as simple as that.

It is as simple as that so far as the motivation is concerned. That is, what moves a person's heart? But, of course, it is infinitely complicated in its working out in the laws of justice in political, economic, and social terms. Christian people have no right to have simplistic solutions to the complex problems of the social order. But they do have a very clear perspective by which those problems can be evaluated. The only way to national unity is the way toward increased justice and greater fairness for the people of the land, that they may deal with one another, forbearing one another, being kindly, affectionate to one another. That is the way that God's praise is shown forth among the nations of the earth. That is what the Bicentennial celebration is all about. And that is something that all citizens can participate in without regard for class, for color, or creed.

But as Christians, we do have a creed. That is, we have a priority in our loyalty. Our trust is finally in God, not in our nation—no matter how just or how proud we may be. Our trust as Christians is in God. It was put in this form by one of our founding fathers who was a Christian. John Adams, you may remember, was a friend of Thomas Jefferson. They had been friends during the colonial period, but they went somewhat different ways politically during the Washington Administration, as one became head of the Federalists and the other the head of the Democratic Party. Despite their political differences, they reestablished that friendship in their old age and deepened it. And they exchanged ideas in their letters. They talked about friends, the weather, politics, life, the meaning of life, faith, and the meaning of faith. Jefferson was a Deist, that is, he believed in a Supreme Being as a rational principle which was often called "universal benevolence." Adams said that faith had to mean more than universal benevolence. Jefferson wrote back, "Well, what is it then?" Adams replied, "Faith means that I rejoice in God and his creation, and I exult in my own existence." Reinhold Niebuhr, commenting on this said, "As I read this I thought that the final phrase ('exulting in one's own existence') sounded somewhat heretical." Then he reminded himself of what the Psalmist said, "I am fearfully and wonderfully made. Marvelous are thy works; and that my soul knoweth right well." "This," Niebuhr concludes, "is classical Christian faith as against the childish corruption of that faith."

The Psalmist says, "I am fearfully and wonderfully made." And he also says, "O clap your hands, all ye people." So on the note of clapping hands, of applauding God, of directing our attention toward him, of rejoicing in him that our celebration may move beyond our own personal, subjective, emotional celebrations toward the greatness of life into our unity as a nation—we pray that we may as a nation come together, as we hope we may as individuals come together, and so embark upon the Bicentennial as citizens of America, and as citizens who are Christians celebrating not simply our nation but celebrating our God.

So we come to the end. The procession is going by. You have your palm branches in your hands. You are in the crowd. Wave! Wave at Jesus! Hosanna! Alleluia! Christ the King comes, an offering so that all men—Christian and non-Christian alike—may come to rejoice in God and their creation. The procession of the King is the process of life. To trust God is to trust life and those forces in it that promise greater life for all men. Then the only way finally to rejoice and to celebrate is not to stay in the crowd as the procession goes by but to join the procession and let your love as a person (which unifies you increasingly) be expressed in justice for your neighbor and for all the sorts and conditions of people who make up this nation.

Then it is not Jesus waving his palm branch back at you as he passes by. He lifts it high ahead of you. As he leads you and you rejoice in life trusting the process, the building of a more fair land, you will help make the national celebration inevitable. It cannot *help* but happen.

> *O, clap your hands, all ye people. Wave your palm branches. Join the procession. Lift up your hearts. Hosanna The King approaches. Get on with your living. This is not only to wave to the glory of God, it is to live to be his glory.*
> *Amen.*
>
> *The King draws nigh now*
> *on the road to Calvary.*
> *We stand hidden in the crowd*
> *in the city with palm branches*
> *in our hands.*

Let us watch him as he draws
to himself from the crowds
   —those who have no hope
   —without position in the world,
   —or chance of any
   —without possessions, or few
   —without work
   —and little prospect of any
   —without savings
   —or dwellings
   —or food
   —or family
   —or friends.
So as we watch you
and watch you draw our
brothers and sisters to you,
we pray to you.
O King, give us the courage to
step out from the protective
coloration of being only
with our own kind,
in our own crowd
   —to be merciful to those
   —in need of mercy
   —kind to those who have
   —known no kindness
   —fair to those whose lot
   —has been an unfair deal.
As we step forward to take our place with,
to identify ourselves with,
to have compassion for the dispossessed,
the hungry and rich in mind, body, or estate
may we be open to your
love and mercy for all men
and so show love and mercy
ourselves.
Help us to be forbearing and forgiving
at home,
with our friends and relations

and all dear to us,
accepting each other as we are
with mercy and good humor.
May our concern for others
burst beyond our homes
into our communities
and our nation
as we deal fairly with
care for each other.
As we share the suffering of others
we share yours
　　—so may we journey
　　—through the city
　　—to Calvary,
and so enter finally into
　　—the glorious joy and hope
　　—of your victory
　　—over all pain and separation
　　—and death
　　—in the power of your resurrection.
May we then celebrate Easter
with a whole heart
because we have celebrated
our common humanity
with the
broken hearted. Amen.

Mystery — Christ — Glory

—⚬⚬⚬—

The Seventeenth Sunday after Pentecost, September 14, 1975

In preparing for the first sermon I was to preach at St. James' Church as rector in September of 1969, I made notes concerning the Epistle for that day. That day was the 16th Sunday after Trinity. By coincidence— or Providence—that is the same day today. I should like to ask you to begin this sermon with me by taking a moment, if you will, to look at the Epistle for today which is on page 212 in the Prayer Book.

[*Editor's note: The text from the 1928 version of the Book of Common Prayer reads: "I desire that ye faint not at my tribulations for you, which is your glory. For this cause I bow my knees unto the Father of our Lord Jesus Christ, of whom the whole family in heaven and earth is named, that he would grant you, according to the riches of his glory, to be strengthened with might by his Spirit in the inner man; that Christ may dwell in your hearts by faith; that ye, being rooted and grounded in love, may be able to comprehend with all saints what is the breadth, and length, and depth, and height; and to know the love of Christ, which passeth knowledge, that ye might be filled with all the fulness of God. Now unto him that is able to do exceeding abundantly above all that we ask or think, according to the power that worketh in us, unto him be glory in the church by Christ Jesus throughout all ages, world without end. Amen." (Ephesians 3:13–21)*].

(We can pass over that first sentence. I'm not sure why any tribulations I have should be your glory; and it has never occurred to me that you might faint dead away because of them. But that is St. Paul.)

The notes follow the Epistle in a very straightforward way. Any minister speaking to the people he is to minister to—those that he comes to live with—he does so for one purpose only: that those people might be strengthened by the spirit of God in their inner life; that in this sense Christ might be yours; that you may, in the relationship, be rooted and grounded in love so that you might understand what God is up to in your life; finally so that you may thank and praise *him,* to whom be the glory.

In attempting to translate that passage of Scripture into our own language and our own situations I went on to say, and these are still the notes, "I am here to serve you—not on your terms or my terms—but God's. There is no use giving you simply what you want or what I want but only what God wants. The way we discover what God wants is as we are open to one another, face the issues of the day outside the church, as well as inside the church, honestly, listen to one another and then do what we believe he wants us to do.

"Therefore, it is a privilege to be invited to come into this family of St. James'. This congregation was here before I came. It will be here after I leave. I hope, simply, that when I leave the life of the Spirit will be stronger.

"The way to strength is that the church be concerned for the city. Our own inner strength grows as we give it away into the lives of men and women who live in the city. So, of course, we have to deal with the issues of society—housing, welfare, drugs, discrimination, education, color.

"This is how the inner strength of the Spirit glorifies God. We go to the root—grounded in God, not in political or social theories, but in God himself."

I will stand by those notes those years ago. Curiously—coincidentally or Providentially—that Epistle was the text of the first sermon I ever preached in my ministry as rector in Grace Church, Amherst, in 1946.

I share this somewhat less than thrilling autobiographical data with you in order to identify one omission in those notes. While it is true that the ministry is essentially to ground the people of God in God, the fact is that Christian people ground their minister in God, as they ground one another. So in preparing to leave this particular family in Christ, I am not prepared to judge the effectiveness of this ministry. As Paul says elsewhere, "with me it is a very small thing that I should be judged by you or by any human court. I do not even judge myself." But I do know that the strengthening of one's inner spirit—my own knowledge of God—has been because of this company—because you shared your spirit. And so you have renewed me. It is that spirit of renewal, of affirming life—of affirming everything in it, including, finally, death, that God is glorified. It is that kind of glorification that holds life together—

that makes it at times just bearable; at other times makes life ecstatic; and at all times makes it worthwhile.

So the sermon in a sense is both a reminder and a "Thank you." It is a reminder of our fundamental and essential nature and to thank you for your ministry. As a result of these years I know better that I ever have before the complementary truths that "there is no health in me" of myself and also that in Christ in me that there is "the hope of glory." That is the gift of the Christian Church—of Christian people to one another. That is the giving of "the means of grace and the hope of glory."* That is what the family of the church is.

One more bit of biographical data. This last summer I re-read all the sermons I preached in this church. It is not a task I would assign either to my best friend—or worst enemy. I shall spare you, this morning, a summary of them. But it was quite clear that there are three convictions that reflect what we have experienced and what at least I have learned. They can be put into three words. (You might wonder if all I have said can be put into three words why I have taken so many words to say them.)

The first word that comes time and time again (either the word itself or implications, moods around the word, reflections about the word), is the word *mystery*. It is not so much saying that life is mystery and then trying to define it, as though definition would capture the meaning of some of the mystery. It is not simply that I am more aware of the mystery of existence than I once was—though that is certainly true, I shudder to think of how much I knew absolutely thirty years ago! Nor is it just realizing that you can never be sure of anything—or almost anything. We don't know what is going to happen tomorrow. We don't know how life is going to turn out. It is jumbled. The unexpected, the surprises always come bursting in on us, especially when we think we have everything . . . and our place figured out. Things turn out differently. Life turns out differently—sometimes better, sometimes worse. Once we think we have control of it, a change takes place. Something happens, sometimes something tragic, sometimes sheer grace, sometimes pain, sometimes joy. Life is just surprises.

I am thinking of mystery in all of these ways, but more than any of them I think of mystery as a way of looking at life. Life is meant to be

---

*These phrases are from 1928 Book of Common Prayer (pp. 6; 19; 23; 33). Not all appear in the 1979 version.

affirmed. Its mystery is to be affirmed. Mystery is not something to be deplored, but applauded. Affirming mystery makes wonder possible: astonishment, expectation, amazement, excitement. It nourishes an expectant attitude, anticipating, watching, waiting. It keeps us humble. We don't own life. We don't own people. We don't own anything. We may be owned by mystery, by life, possessed by it. We belong to it. We can trust it, but it is not ours, and we do not control it. The incredible wonder of nature or of beauty—a painting, a work of art, music, a person, a soul. The mysterious, powerful way by which people respond to life. Mysterious, graceful, doing more than they ever thought that they could do. That's mysterious. Mystery makes worship possible, and adoration.

We don't know very much about the essential nature of our existence. We don't know, for example, why we are here. We may, through science, learn more and more about material aspects of life and nature, how atoms are put together, what they can do, for example, but its essential nature, or their essential nature, why they are here and exist, why we are here—that continues to escape us. It is all terribly elusive. It has to be wrestled through generation after generation. What my father thought is interesting but not compelling. You have to know what your fathers taught but you work it through and your children work it through on their terms, not on yours. We don't own them. That is a pilgrimage. Generation after generation is a mystery. We know so little. T. S. Eliot put it this way:

> There are only hints and guesses,
> Hints followed by guesses; and the rest
> Is prayer, observation, discipline, thought and action.
> The hint half guessed, the gift half understood is Incarnation.

Incarnation: *Christ.* That is the second word. Life, death, resurrection—Truth revealed in a person; the nature of ultimate truth—beyond the mystery—revealed in a person. Truth, being, existence, creation—in him. Truth is revealed in a person, in personality, in Christ. A person is always known in our meeting, trusting, loving, accepting one another. This is how we come to know another person. So Christ brings in his person the nature of the truth of God. Love is born, killed, rises again. It is always coming back, no matter what happens. Trusting him, meeting him, turning to him, trying to live in him, with him, waiting for him, expecting him. He comes. The person, the man who loves you personally. That truth is a great mystery. It's known only by faith. God is known never by thought alone but only by love. Meet him. Trust him. Love him.

So, the final word: *Glory.* The Epistle ends, "unto him be glory in the church by Christ Jesus throughout all ages, world without end. Amen." Glory, praise, thanksgiving, honor, worship, adoration—all words which try to capture that sense of being caught up, of being possessed, captured by a spirit which carries us, moves us into another dimension where our center is no longer in ourself but out there—transcendent, beyond us—to which we belong. The nature of that center becomes our nature. *We* become more glorious. When we say of a sunset, even just a sunset, "My, that sunset is glorious," what we mean to say is that we are lifted by it—our hearts are lifted—we are strengthened. There is beauty there to which we belong. Some of that, sometimes, rubs off on us. Sometimes that is the only eternal we can touch, see, hold on to. To say to another person "I love you" is glorious. It means your center is no longer just in yourself. You belong to another. It is to be renewed.

So we glorify God. We praise him and in the act of praising, participate in him, become part of his nature. And in the process of affirming him, we are affirmed. To say "Glory to God" is to say "Glory"—to say "Yes" to ourselves, to one another, to our existence. To be in glory is to be in God.

So the conclusion of that text and the sermon: "To him be the glory in the church by Christ Jesus" is simply to say that the mystery which surrounds us, illuminated by the love we are given one another imperfectly, is the way things really are. That is the way it is in life for all of us, a little bit; that is the way it is in the fellowship of the church by Christ Jesus and his spirit, at our best; and that is the way it is in eternity—throughout all ages, world without end. Amen.

All Saints' Day Celebration

—⚶—

All Saints' Sunday,
November 2, 1975—Final sermon
as rector of St. James' Church

What to say on such a day as All Saints' Day? To mention memories? Memories of pain and joy? Memories of battles, some won, some lost? Memories of death and life? Fun times, times of agony? Memories that exhilarate, memories that depress? Memories of love shared, embracing? Memories of not being able to love enough, care enough, share enough? Memories of strength surging and memories of emptiness?

We are at any time and certainly at such a time as All Saints' Day, this day, we *are* our memories. What we call to mind is who we are. "Call to mind" is perhaps not quite the accurate phrase for that implies intellectual remembering, an act of deciding what we shall recall and what we shall try to blot from our memory. It is not events that determine who we are; good events over against bad events. It is, rather, the sum total of all the experiences we go through; the spirit that has permeated them all—the bad as well as the good—that molds us. We are who we are because of everything we have been through—remembered and forgotten, the shameful and bitter—as the glorious and sweet—the unconscious as the conscious, the spirit moving through our psychic depths as well as the partial recall of our reason—all of *that* has formed us. It is what has happened to us, and what our response has been to what has happened. Our response that was rooted in bad reasons as well as good reasons. Reasons we understood as well as reasons still hidden from us that has brought us to this day.

Now in retrospect we can hardly distinguish the good from the bad, or we withhold judgment from such evaluation for often the bad and the good reverse themselves—often the pain and the joy rise out of the same experience, the same source, two sides of the same. Darkness and light in retrospect become alike. We have moved, we have been moved, from the darkness and the mists of our past into the light and the shadows and the ambiguities of our present and our present selves.

Memories, then, we may cherish—we do cherish them—and we thank God for them. We thank God for them because only so is it possible for us ever to thank the people who gave those memories to us and made them possible. Without those people we would not be who we are. On such a day as this in such a place we can only thank God who has given those people to us—all of those people—those we have loved and those we have had trouble even putting up with—because it is they who have carried us, shaping us, reshaping, renewing, reforming, refining us.

So here we are—just as we are—with them, today, *celebrating*. There is no other word possible—celebrating, applauding, clapping our hands, our spirits applauding, celebrating with our entire beings—ourselves clapping. Because of our memories we can celebrate the present and if we can celebrate the present, then we can look into the future with hope. Or perhaps better, we can trust the future. We can trust the future because we have cause for rejoicing in the present. We can rejoice in the present because we bring into this day and this service our memories. We can celebrate now so that we may move into the future with trust and with confidence, and hope and expectancy and excitement.

Indeed the quality of our celebration, the way we give thanks to God, the way we respond to him now and try to live in him now and rejoice in him now, all of that assures us that future. It confirms us in the future no matter what happens. Or in him, rather, the future is confirmed. That future in him, no matter what happens to us, is glorious because God is glorious—and we only know him now.

The word that Christians use to describe that future is *heaven*. The meaning of that word, as the meaning of all words of this character, is the meaning that we give it. Our experiences, our responses to those experiences, the spirit with which we accept and appropriate for ourselves everything that happens to us and live through those experiences in his spirit—all of them—all of that determines what heaven is. The quality of life on earth as just men and women gathered together going through all the experiences human beings go through both determines and reflects the quality of life in heaven—that is, the quality of life in God.

So when we celebrate as we do on this All Saints' Day we are celebrating our life in heaven, remembering particularly our living in love with those who have gone through the experience of death and now live, as we say, "in heaven." We celebrate our lives and loves with them now on earth as we shall in heaven forever.

There are two grounds for Christians to put this kind of meaning into that word, heaven. They both rise out of our present life and our own experience and you already know them. I mention them, not to persuade you—no person can ever persuade another of the reality of heaven—but simply to remind you of your own experiences as human beings who have been bound together with others in loving relationships, your present experience and the experiences that you call to mind through your memories. And to say: *trust those*. Trust that spirit. Trust the quality of that relationship where you have lived and loved and where you are presently living and loving because that is the quality of eternal life.

So take the hand you hold and caress it. Take the yearning you have and embrace it. Take the tears you have for another. Take the pain that bursts forth and breaks when love is broken. Take the grief when a loved one dies. Take the agony of spirit that prompts your caring and the agony because you can never care enough. Take the longing when the ones you love go, and you know you have to lose them and let them go. Take the compassion for your loved ones who suffer when you would—but cannot. Take their suffering upon yourself. Take the meeting and surprises of meeting the people you love—that instant recognition from eternity. Take the excitement of anticipating that meeting, that reunion, the joy of meeting and being met—surprised by joy forever. Take the joy-bearers in your life. Take the spirit surging and springing up within you when you find yourselves spontaneously caring, loving, agonizing, embracing and set free from possessing those persons you meet in the spirit of love.

Take that spirit that moves through all these relationships and *trust* it. That is one ground for eternal life. The trusting can only come out of the depths of your heart and of your love. That is your living *now* in heaven and trusting that quality forever—through all the experiences of life including the end of physical life. The spirit lives.

There is another reason—Jesus Christ—as simple as that. He is, he says, the resurrection and the life. To know him, he says, is eternal life. In my father's house, he says, there are many rooms. And when I go away from you, he says, I am going to prepare a place for you, that where I am you too may be. Nothing, he says, nothing—nothing in life or in death can ever separate you from my *love*—ever.

So—trust him. To trust the quality of life within you which is the spirit of love moving through those personal relationships—where you really love and trust it—is to trust him. They are both the same. The relationship with those you love and with him, and the trusting of it—that is heaven.

When we go into the unknown land of the future we go with the Lord who is known in the present. That is heaven. We go into that future one step at a time. The only step we have to take is today.

Let me now conclude. Separations come in life. People we love go away, come back, go away, die. And when they go away, we die a little bit ourselves. We do if we love them. All such little deaths are part of God's preparing us for the deaths of people we love, and for our own death. These are part of life so that together we may be raised to a new life, with new power, and renewed, eternal love surging in heaven.

Curiously enough we grow closer to people we love as we grow closer to God. The absence of people we love brings them closer to us when we go deeper into God. We live with them more intimately in the spirit as we trust and live the spirit within us and around us where we are. The greatest thing we can do for them is to put them in the spirit of the loving God and live more closely in the same spirit in our own hearts. The more we do in God, for God, the more we do for them. The more we live in him, the more we live with them. The more we love him, the more we love them. The miracle is—they know it and we know it. They are helped to live with us in that love eternally in heaven, and in the same heavenly love today.

That is why memories on such a day as this, of our life together in love help us to celebrate this day. Our celebration is the celebration of Jesus Christ and his love from which we are never separated, from which those we love are never separated, and which as we love him assures us of our life with one another in heaven.

So on this day of all the saints whom we remember, let us pray:

O Lord God, who in your Son Jesus Christ have shown us most fully of your love, bless and keep, we pray you, those men, women, and children who also are bearers of your love to us and whom we remember this day. May we help them, not hinder them, in their journey through life, through death, through new life.

Bring us, we pray you, bring us all safe at last to your heavenly home, where we shall live completely in your love and with one another by the strength and in the spirit of him who travels with us, from the past into the present, into the future forever, your son, Jesus Christ our Lord. Amen.

John B. Coburn
1914–2009

—〰—

A Timeline

Born at Danbury, Connecticut, September 27, 1914

Wooster School, Danbury, Connecticut

Princeton University, BA, 1936

Robert College as a teacher, 1936–1939

Married Ruth Barnum, May 26, 1941

Graduated Union Theological Seminary, New York, BD, 1942

Ordained priest, 1943

Assistant Minister, Grace Church, New York City, 1942–1944

Chaplain in U.S. Naval Reserve, 1944

Rector Grace Church, Amherst, Massachusetts, and Chaplain of the college, 1946–1953

Dean of Trinity Cathedral, Newark, New Jersey, 1953–1957

Dean at Episcopal Theological School, Cambridge, Massachusetts, 1957–1967

Teacher, Urban League Street Academy, Harlem, 1968–1969

Chosen Rector of St. James' Church, New York City, May 17, 1969

Preached first sermon at St. James', September 28, 1969

Preached last sermon at St. James', November 2, 1975

Resigned as rector effective, November 2, 1975

Consecrated Bishop of Massachusetts, October 2, 1976

Retired as Bishop of Massachusetts, 1986

Died, August 8, 2009, only a few weeks short of his 95th birthday

---

John B. Coburn's Association with National Church

Deputy to the General Convention
    from Diocese of Newark   1955
    from Diocese of Massachusetts   1961, 1964

Elected President, House of Deputies
    from Diocese of Massachusetts   1967
    from Diocese of New York   1970
    from Diocese of New York   1973
    from Diocese of New York   1976

Elected Bishop of Massachusetts   May 31, 1975

Consecrated Bishop of Massachusetts   October 2, 1976

Retired as active bishop   1986

St. James' Church in 1969

O n May 17, 1969, when John B. Coburn was chosen rector, the senior warden was James M. Hubball and the junior warden was Jarvis Cromwell. Clifford Michel was a vestryman and chairman of the search committee. Arthur Lee Kinsolving, John Coburn's predecessor as rector, had suggested John's name to Cliff Michel as a good candidate. Vestryman Sims Farr had also received high praise about him from John Butler, rector of Trinity, Wall Street, and from Bob Potter, a trustee of the Episcopal Theological Seminary when John B. Coburn was dean there.

In the fall of 1969, Hubball and Cromwell retired as wardens of St. James' and were succeeded by Michel and Farr as senior and junior wardens, respectively. In November 1970, I was elected to the vestry. This was the last election at St. James' with a single slate of nominees for warden and vestryman chosen by a committee of vestrymen.

During the following year, at the suggestion of the rector, who believed that the procedure to choose the vestry should be more open and involve more parishioners, a committee of four vestry was appointed to review the election process. The committee consisted of Messrs. Michel, Farr, Held, and myself. Also a group of parishioners not on the vestry and led by Nancy Mullon and Liz Susman actively promoted the need for change. Although there was opposition, the vestry finally approved a new system which was followed in the fall of 1971. The two significant changes were that the nominating committee consisted of equal numbers of vestry members and parishioners who were not on the vestry; and the committee selected twice as many nominees for vestry as there were vacancies. Election of warden received a single slate. The parish accepted this change, and it remains this way today. This was the first significant structural change in the parish under John Coburn's rectorship and would not have occurred without his strong support.